Pinterest Kickstart

Heather Morris
David Todd

The **McGraw·Hill** Companies

Cataloging-in-Publication Data is on file with the Library of Congress

McGraw-Hill books are available at special quantity discounts to use as premiums and sales promotions, or for use in corporate training programs. To contact a representative, please e-mail us at bulksales@mcgraw-hill.com.

Pinterest Kickstart

Pinterest Growth Chart graphic in Chapter 12 used with permission from Statista Inc.

1 2 3 4 5 6 7 8 9 0   DOC DOC   1 0 9 8 7 6 5 4 3 2

ISBN   978-0-07-180559-9
MHID   0-07-180559-1

SPONSORING EDITOR	COPY EDITOR	ILLUSTRATION
Megg Morin	Claire Splan	Cenveo Publisher Services
EDITORIAL SUPERVISOR	**PROOFREADER**	**ART DIRECTOR, COVER**
Janet Walden	Julie Searls	Jeff Weeks
PROJECT MANAGER	**INDEXER**	
Vastavikta Sharma, Cenveo Publisher Services	Claire Splan	
	PRODUCTION SUPERVISOR	
ACQUISITIONS COORDINATOR	James Kussow	
Stephanie Evans	**COMPOSITION**	
TECHNICAL EDITOR	Cenveo Publisher Services	
Jill Duffy		

For Finley and Callum

About the Authors

Heather Morris is a technical writer and editor who has written easy-to-use technology guides. Her publications include *The Healthy Mac, Scanning and Editing Your Old Photos, Researching Your Family History Online*, and *Starting Up an Online Business*.

David Todd is a seasoned social networking early adopter and avid user of Facebook, LinkedIn, Yammer, and Pinterest. He analyzes Internet content, writes textbooks for young learners of English, and stays ahead of the social networking curve.

About the Technical Editor

Jill Duffy is a writer and software analyst at *PC Magazine*. She also writes a weekly column about staying organized in a digital world at www.pcmag.com/get-organized.

CONTENTS

PART I

Learn About Pinterest and How to Use It Effectively

PART II

Explore Individual Project Ideas

PART III

Discover Collaborative Project Ideas

ACKNOWLEDGMENTS

The authors would like to thank the following people for their help creating this book:

- Megg Morin, Stephanie Evans, and Janet Walden for their enthusiasm, feedback, and ongoing support during each stage of the book

- Neil Salkind of the Salkind Literary Agency for his ongoing support and encouragement

- Jill Duffy for her helpful feedback and suggestions

- Claire Splan for her meticulous review of the manuscript and preparation of the index

- Julie Searls for proofreading the book

- Vastavikta Sharma for coordinating the production of the book

INTRODUCTION

*P*interest Kickstart is an all-in-one guide to the Internet's hottest new social web site. The book takes you from registration to planning complex functional pin boards that help you maximize the potential of this flexible site.

In addition to providing simple how-to information on using the site, *Pinterest Kickstart* shows you dozens of ways you can use the site with individual project ideas. All ideas are supported with real-life examples you can check out at http://pinterest.com/heatheranddave/.

In Part I of this book, you'll learn what Pinterest is and how you can use it:

- Chapter 1 tells you a little about the arrival of Pinterest on the social media scene and the many ways people are using it. You'll learn about some of the basics of the site, how to register for Pinterest, and some of the rules.

- Chapter 2 shows you how to add the Pin It button and create and add content to your account. The chapter discusses finding great sources of content for your boards including images you find on the Internet, videos, or your own photographs and art.

- Chapter 3 walks you through customizing your Pinterest page, including managing your email notification settings, changing your display settings, and linking personal web sites and other social media accounts.

- Chapter 4 explains how to take advantage of the central social element of the site by inviting friends via email and adding friends from other social media sites. You'll also learn how to reference and mention friends in pins.

- Chapter 5 explores Pinterest's mobile applications and the best third-party web applications that leverage your Pinterest content. You'll learn how to use the Pinterest mobile site in conjunction with the mobile applications, add Pin It buttons to cell phones and tablets, and create pins without an image or video.

In Part II you'll see 15 different ideas for individual Pinterest projects:

- Chapter 6 offers you ideas for making boards focused on things you like, places you love, and special people in your life. It also makes suggestions for consolidating your existing photo and video collections within Pinterest.

- Chapter 7 shows you how to make boards for your home. You'll learn how to use the web site for planning projects like craft activities, home improvement, and gardening. You'll see how to use Pinterest to consolidate recipe collections and plan family meals.

- Chapter 8 explores ways to bring Pinterest into your work and study life. You'll see how you can use Pinterest for educational planning, and how you can use the site to visualize your educational reading lists. You'll also learn how you can stand out to recruiters by transferring your résumé to Pinterest.

In Part III you'll see more ideas for using Pinterest for collaborative projects:

- Chapter 9 guides you through creating Pinterest boards for communities and clubs. You'll learn how you can showcase collections, integrate existing web sites and social sites into your boards, and build an online community.

- Chapter 10 shows you how to build boards for smaller audiences. You'll see ideas for shortlisting titles for a book club, planning group exercise and parties, building a wish list, and running a scavenger hunt.

- Chapter 11 explores various ideas for raising awareness of issues and events. You'll learn how to use Pinterest to promote and plan events. You'll also see ways to create boards dedicated to certain topics of interest and how to use Pinterest to raise awareness of an important issue.

- Chapter 12 walks you through ideas and strategies for using Pinterest for your business. You'll learn how to get your business on Pinterest, ways to develop an online following, and how you can run a promotion.

Conventions Used in This Book

Now You Know   The Now You Know sidebars provide deeper detail on a topic or specifics for accomplishing a task.

Tip   Tips help you make the most of Pinterest by offering shortcuts or ways to streamline and super-charge your Pinterest experience.

Note   Notes aim to draw your attention to supplemental information, background steps, or additional requirements.

Caution   Keep a sharp eye out for the Caution icon to help you steer clear of potential pitfalls or problems that may lie ahead.

Part I
Learn About Pinterest and How to Use It Effectively

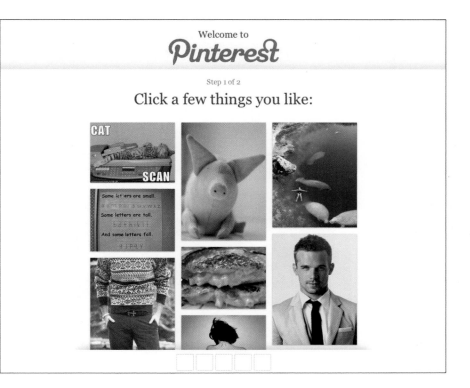

1

What Is Pinterest and Why Use It?

The exponential growth of Pinterest has been the topic of media buzz for some time and the site has been heralded as the next big thing in social media. If you somehow missed the hundreds of articles on the topic, maybe your social-media savvy friends have been raving about it and urging you to join in. So what's all the fuss about?

In this chapter we look at what Pinterest is, and why you might want to join the millions of users who are enjoying and benefitting from this dynamic site. We also explain how to join the site and some of the basics about what joining Pinterest actually entails.

A Short History of Pinterest

Pinterest started out with the simple aim of encouraging users to collect and share images they find on the Web. This straightforward idea has developed into one of the most popular and fastest-growing social sites in history. And, if you think about it, it's not hard to see why. We all browse the Internet each day and come across things we find interesting, beautiful, useful, or even amusing.

Pinterest gives you one place, your own web site really, to pin all these visual bookmarks. It differs from other social media sites in that it focuses on content you find interesting, rather than simply connecting you with friends or relatives (who you may not always find interesting). You can collect and organize your finds onto boards. A board is analogous to an

3

actual pin board—a place to pin a collection of images or ideas you want to keep track of for later. You can share your boards with friends and family, or simply gather things for no reason other than you think they're cool. In addition, small businesses can use Pinterest to showcase their products and services and drive traffic to their sites. While you'll see mostly images on the site, there are several crafty ways you can pin text and video as well.

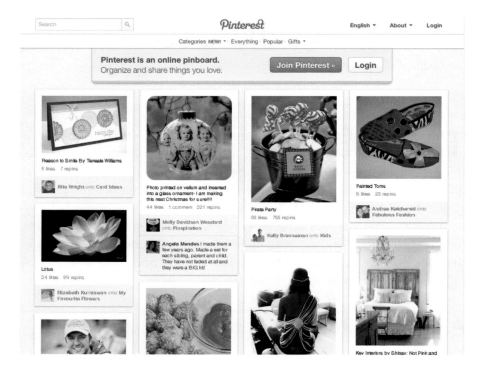

Pinterest's growth has been phenomenal. The service launched as an invitation-only beta site in March 2010—in tech industry–speak this means it was considered complete enough to release to the public in a low-key way, but was definitely not a final polished product. By December 2011, it had grown to a massive 11 million users. In the U.S., the vast majority of users are women and much of the content on the site reflects interests you might typically think of as "female." However, Pinterest is an international site and the breakdown of users varies. In the U.K., for example, the majority of users appears to be male—at least at the time of this writing. Like most new social networks, Pinterest quickly added a mobile dimension to its offering in the form of an iOS (Apple) application and Android app that allow users to access the site on their smartphones or tablets.

Learn About How You Can Use Pinterest

We look at the numerous ways you can use Pinterest in some detail throughout this book. Pinterest isn't merely about finding attractive images, and you don't even have to limit yourself to pinning images. You can also pin videos you find on YouTube and Vimeo, snippets of text, and quotes—just about anything that can be contained in a visual format. Here are some of the more common uses of Pinterest:

- Browse the millions of boards already on Pinterest to get ideas or learn something new.
- Create boards for yourself about topics that interest you or around your personal goals like improving your diet or starting an exercise regime.
- Plan events like birthdays, weddings, or dinner parties.
- Find other users who share your interests or hobbies and share content and ideas.
- Work collaboratively with others to build and curate a board around common interests or goals.
- Shop for home items, craft products, gadgets, and more.
- Use your smartphone or tablet to find inspiration while you are out and about.
- Pin work-related content or use Pinterest to help you find a new job.
- Drive new traffic to your blog or web site.
- Share popular content from your own business web site and connect with existing and potential customers.
- Gather ideas for redecorating your home or designing a tattoo.

The possibilities are truly endless. Once you log into the site and see what other users are up to, you'll doubtless develop a few more ideas yourself. After you get started, the biggest problem isn't going to be coming up with things to do on Pinterest. In fact, you're more likely to struggle to find time to do all the things you want with the site.

Understand Pins

A *pin* is an image you find on the Internet or upload yourself from your computer. You can pin images from just about any web site when you install the Pin It button. The Pin It button is a tool that you add to your browser's toolbar. A pin grabbed from a web site automatically links back to the original site. You can also pin videos you find on the Web—maybe a how-to video on how to complete a craft, or a video of your favorite comedian doing his spiel. Finally, with third-party tools, you can create text pins to add to your boards—things like favorite quotes from a book or your very own Top Ten list to share with others.

The example pin shown here is an image found on a site that sells a variety of wall stencils for home décor. If another user on Pinterest wants to find out more about a pin, they click the image and go directly to the original site. Other users can "like" your pin (much as one does on Facebook), comment on a pin, or repin it to their own Pinterest account. The original site, in this case, royaldesignstudio.com, displays at the bottom of the pin to credit its original source.

Moroccan wall stencil

4 likes   8 repins

royaldesignstudio.com

Understand Boards

A *board* on Pinterest is a place to organize all the pins you collect while browsing Pinterest and the Internet, or that you've created yourself with your computer or camera. The major advantage of Pinterest boards is that you can create as many boards as you want to organize your pins into logical categories. You can sort your pins into categories generated by Pinterest including Design, Education, Food & Drink, Humor, Photography, Sports, Weddings, and many more. You can also create your own boards based on your interest or hobbies.

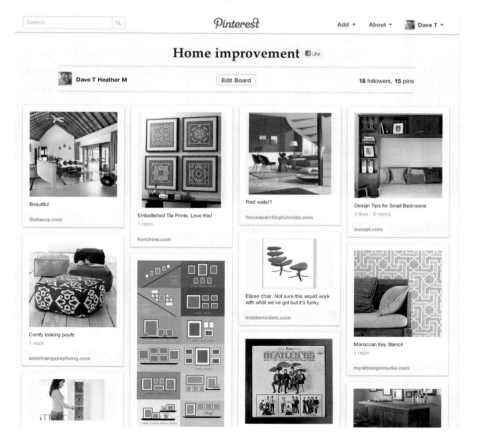

When you pin an image from your browser, you can select which board you want to pin it to or create a new board on the spot. For example, say you happen across a good brownie recipe and don't yet have a board created for food. When you click the Pin It button, you can choose to create a new board called Sweets or Chocolate Goodies for that pin to go to.

Join Pinterest

Joining Pinterest can be as simple as entering your email address and creating a password for the site. Before the site opened up registration to everyone in this manner in August 2012, you had to receive an invitation to join *and* have an existing social networking account through either Facebook or Twitter. You can still register with your existing Facebook or Twitter account, but you no longer need an invitation before you can sign up. We'll look at the two options for joining Pinterest in this next section.

Join Pinterest with Your Email Account

The easiest way to join Pinterest is by registering with your existing email address and creating a password. The process of joining will take you through several screens where you'll enter some of your personal information and also select pin categories on the site, like Education, Photography, or Travel that you're interested in viewing.

To join Pinterest:

1. Go to www.pinterest.com and click the Join Pinterest button.

2. The site will show you some sample images, as shown in Figure 1-1. Select five or more that you like by clicking them. Scroll down the page if needed to find more. When you've clicked a few images, Pinterest will display a Continue button at

Figure 1-1   *Click images you are interested in seeing on Pinterest.*

the bottom. Completing this step helps Pinterest establish the type of content you are interested in. For example, if you click an image of the latest smartphone or other attractive gadget, Pinterest keeps tabs on the fact that you are interested in content from the Geek category.

3. Click Continue and click the Sign Up With Your Email link.

4. On the next page enter a username, as shown here. You can use any combination of letters and numbers up to 15 characters long. If the username you want is already taken, try variations of your desired name by adding a middle initial or series of numbers.

Create your account

Username

Email Address

Upload your Photo Password

First Name

Last Name

By creating an account, I accept Pinterest's **Terms of Service** and **Privacy Policy.**

Create Account

5. Enter your email address and create a password. The password you type here will be the password for your new Pinterest account.

6. Type your first and last name in the final two fields. The name that you enter here will be the name that other Pinterest users will see on your profile and on content you pin. If you want to maintain some of your privacy, you can use a nickname or just include an initial for your first or last name.

7. Add your photo or an image if you want. You can do this by clicking the Upload Your Photo button and uploading an image from your computer.

8. Click Create Account when you've finished entering all your information.

You will see a banner at the top of the Pinterest site after you sign in asking you to verify your email address. You should do this by logging into your email and locating the message from Pinterest asking you to verify your address. Once you've opened the message, click the Verify your email button in the message and you'll be taken back to the Pinterest home page.

Join Pinterest with Your Facebook or Twitter Account

You can also sign up for Pinterest with an existing Facebook or Twitter account. There are a few advantages to logging in with either of these. First, it makes it easy to find people you know and to see how they are using the site and the types of content they're pinning, which can be helpful when you first start out. You can also share your Pinterest content on your Facebook Timeline or feed, and tweet pins to your Twitter followers. We explore some of the ways you can use these social sites together in Chapter 4. For now, we'll show you how to use them to join Pinterest. We've used Facebook as our example, but the process will be similar with your Twitter account.

1. Go to www.pinterest.com and click Join Pinterest.

2. The site will show you some sample images (see Figure 1-1, shown earlier). Select five or more images that you like by clicking them. Scroll down the page if needed to find more. When you've clicked enough images, Pinterest will display a Continue button at the bottom. Completing this step helps Pinterest establish the type of content you are interested in.

3. Click Continue and click the Facebook button. If you are already logged into Facebook on your browser, you'll see the screen in Figure 1-2. If you're not logged into your Facebook account, you'll be prompted to log in with your username and password.

4. Click Go To App and you'll be taken to a screen (similar to the one shown with step 4 in the previous section) where you can create your account.

5. Enter a username and create a password for your new Pinterest account. Your username can be any combination of letters and numbers. If the name you want is taken, try variations of your desired name by adding a middle initial or series of numbers.

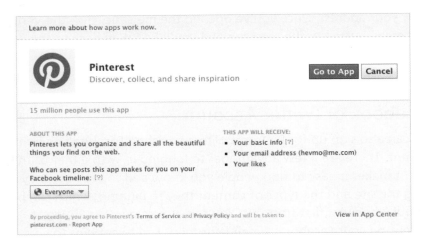

Figure 1-2   *Join Pinterest through your Facebook account.*

6. Enter your first and last name in the final two fields. The name that you enter here will be the name that other Pinterest users will see on your profile and on content you pin. If you want to maintain some of your privacy, you can use a nickname or just include an initial for your first or last name.

7. Upload a new image if you wish or use your existing Facebook photo.

8. Click Create Account and you'll be taken to the main Pinterest page.

 Keep the check box selected next to Follow Recommended Friends if you want to see pins from your Facebook friends. You'll automatically follow them and see the content they pin. We'll discuss more about following, etc. in Chapter 4.

Now You Know — Linking the Wrong Facebook or Twitter Account to Pinterest

If you have only one Windows or Mac OS X user account set up on your computer but have more than one person using it, you may run into problems linking Pinterest to your social networking site. If another user forgot to log out of Facebook, for example, *their* Facebook page will be automatically linked to *your* new Pinterest account. The best way to avoid this is to create separate user accounts on your Windows PC or Mac but, if you haven't, you can remedy the problem fairly quickly by doing the following:

1. Once you are signed into your new Pinterest account, hover your cursor over your username and select Settings.

2. Move the slider next to Login With Facebook (or Twitter) to Off.

3. Open a new tab in your browser and go to Facebook or Twitter, and make sure the other user is logged out. Now log into your Facebook or Twitter account in the same browser.

4. Return to Pinterest's Settings and move the slider next to Login With Facebook (or Twitter) to On.

5. Click Save at the bottom of the page.

Be Aware of Who Can See Your Pins

Pinterest is a public site and anyone who uses it can view your boards and pins. There has been a push from the user community for a private board option but, at present, no such option exists. It's important when you begin that you are aware of the fact that anyone can see your content. With that in mind, you may want to think carefully about whether to include images of children or other people without their knowledge. There might be other types of images you don't want to include as well.

Understand Pinning Etiquette

If you have any experience on social networking sites, then you probably know that they can sometimes prompt heated or colorful exchanges between users. The ethos behind Pinterest is somewhat different.

Pinterest encourages users to be respectful to others when leaving comments or asking questions about pins. It also encourage users to "be authentic." In other words, pin things that you genuinely find interesting or beautiful and reflect your personal taste, rather than using the site to promote yourself or find followers. Good etiquette also includes crediting the sources of your pins (more on that in the next section). Finally, though its policy doesn't state so explicitly, Pinterest probably isn't the venue to engage in heated philosophical debate or to try to convert other people to your own way of thinking. The predominant vibe of the site is more along the lines of "hey, this is cool!"

Note that there are valid uses for businesses on Pinterest but the same sort of etiquette advice applies equally to an organization. There are hundreds of businesses on Pinterest connecting with customers and sharing content that customers enjoy. Creating an entire board out of pins from your business is not encouraged but there are several other ways you can creatively use Pinterest to connect with customers and market your business; we'll explore that in more detail in Chapter 12.

Learn About Copyright and Sources

Trawling through the Web for images for your board can be a lot of fun, but you should be aware of some restrictions on what you can use, especially around copyrighted content. Think about it from the perspective of professional photographers, designers, or others who devote themselves to creating beautiful images. They may not want their image shared or otherwise reproduced across the Internet without their knowledge or permission. In fact, reproducing content onto your Pinterest page without permission is a violation of copyright law. When in doubt, contact the content owner to check that you can use the image.

 If you have a pin that violates the copyright of the owner, the pin can be reported and removed. If you have a number of pins reported for violating copyright, your Pinterest account could be suspended or removed altogether.

To protect copyright, Pinterest offers web site owners an opt-out option to prevent people from pinning their images. These may include sites that display the original work of photographers or designers but there are other businesses and individuals who may prevent you from using an image. Note that any images containing watermarks are copyrighted and not suitable for use. You may find that you are prevented from pinning images from certain sites and get a message "This site does not allow pinning to Pinterest." If you run across this message, you know that the web site owner has opted out and that site's content is not something you can pin. However, don't simply assume that if a site doesn't have an opt-out tag enabled that you can use the images.

 Avoid using the images from image-only search results on Google or Yahoo! when looking for content to pin. If you do an image search, be sure to click through to the original page to see if it's a suitable image, and also to ensure the original source is properly cited.

Now that you've been cautioned about the perils of pinning content you haven't created, we have some good news—there are plenty of excellent web sites that you can use as sources of pinspiration. At present, many retailers proudly display the Pin It button, and actually encourage users to pin their content (knowing as they do that these pins drive visitors to their sites, and such visits can generate money). The number of sites with the Pin It button will continue to expand but here are just a few of the most popular sites that you can use as sources for your Pinterest boards or that already have Pin It buttons added to their pages next to the other social site buttons:

- Amazon.com
- Etsy.com
- Sunset.com
- Aeropostale.com
- Zappos.com
- Potterybarn.com
- Williams-Sonoma.com

In order to see the Pin It buttons for these sites, you have to click through to an individual product page. For example, search for a book on Amazon and then click the link for the book. The Pin It button displays on the right side of the book's product page.

2

Start Using Pinterest

N ow that you have an account and more of a feel for what Pinterest
has to offer, it's time to dive into the site and start creating pins
and boards you'll love. In this chapter we take a look at some of the
features of your Pinterest account and how to use the built-in tools to
create content for your own page by repinning images from the site,
finding things on the Internet, or uploading your own images.

Explore Pinterest

Pinterest has an attractive layout and a straightforward set of tools that
you use to pin and organize the things you find. However, the first time
you log in you may be unsure about what you see, and where some of
the content is coming from. In this section we briefly review some of
the features of the main Pinterest page and how you navigate them to
your own Pinterest page.

Explore the Main Pinterest Page

After you complete the registration process, you go straight to
Pinterest's main page. This page will have several pins that you can
browse through. The pins you see on the main page are from other
users that you are following (see Figure 2-1). Pinterest automatically
has you follow a number of users based on the categories you "liked"
when you first logged in. This pin feed will appear each time you log in
and, depending on the activity level of the other pinners, change daily

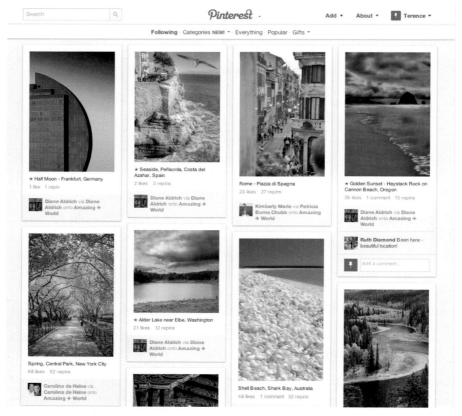

Figure 2-1   *The main page of Pinterest with a feed of pins*

as they pin new content. It's a good way to see how the site works and to get a sense of what other people are pinning.

As you connect with more of your friends on Pinterest or find new people to follow, their pins will display in the pin feed as well. You can see what your friends are up to on Pinterest and follow other users who share your interests.

Many of the social features on Pinterest are activated when you either point your cursor at a pin or click a pin. For example, when you hover your cursor over a pin, you'll see the Repin, Like, and Comment buttons appear. If you hover your cursor over another pinner's name, a link will appear. Click the link to go to that person's Pinterest page to see other content they've pinned.

See What Is on Your Page

Your page really is *your* page with your own Internet address (URL), which you can proudly share with family and friends. Your URL will be pinterest.com/*yourusername*/ and any boards you create will be added to your address. To get to your page from the main page, click once on your name in the upper-right corner of the page.

Pinterest automatically creates a few boards for you based on the categories you liked the first time you logged into the site. For example, if you clicked Food & Drink, you'll have a Food & Drink board waiting for you to add content to it. These boards are where you pin the cool stuff you find while browsing the Web or clicking through other boards on Pinterest.

If you look at the top of your boards, you'll see that you are already following a number of people (these are the people whose pins you see in the main feed). There is also a Followers section at the top of the page. If you have friends already on the site, then you may even have a follower or two!

To return to the main Pinterest page, click the red Pinterest icon at the top of the page.

Create a Unique Board

The default boards that Pinterest generates are very broad in nature, and you may have a more specific idea about content you want to pin. For example, if you chose Gardening as an interest, you may be specifically interested in Japanese gardens or perhaps organic vegetable gardens. Often the best boards are the ones with the most specific content. Boards with broader categories can fill up quickly with pins and be difficult to navigate.

To add a unique board, follow these steps:

1. Click Add at the top of your Pinterest page.

2. Click Create a Board.

3. Enter a specific name for your board (as shown in Figure 2-2).

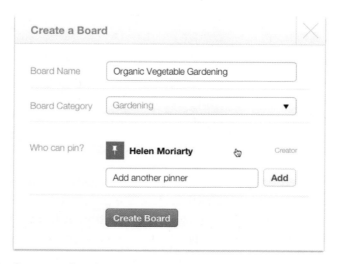

Figure 2-2   *Create a unique board.*

4. Click the drop-down menu and select a category for the board. The category will help other pinners who share your interest find what you pin. If you can't find an exact category for what you have in mind, select Other at the bottom of the list.

5. Click Create Board.

If you have more board ideas in mind, just repeat these steps to create a new board.

You can also change the name of your board or its category at any time. Maybe you started a board for desserts or family meals that evolved into more of a children's party food board with fun, child-friendly recipes and treats. To learn more about editing a board's name and other information, see "Customize Your Boards" in Chapter 3. Before you create too many boards though, you'll probably want to find some pins; we'll tackle that next.

 By default, you are the only person who can add pins to your boards. If you like, you can let friends pin also. We'll show you how to do this in Chapter 4 and will explore some of the ways you can use shared boards.

Add the Pin It Button to Your Browser

The Pin It button allows you to take an image from a web site and add it to one of your boards. It also automatically includes the link (URL) so that the original source is properly credited. You add the button directly to your browser's Favorites or Bookmarks Bar—depending on which browser and operating system you're using. While many web sites already have the Pin It button embedded within them, you'll need this tool for the many thousands more that don't. The button is supported in all major browsers including Internet Explorer, Firefox, Chrome, and Safari.

To determine how to add the tool to your specific browser, click About at the top of the Pinterest page and select Pin It Button from the drop-down menu. You'll be taken to the instructions for your browser, which is detected automatically by Pinterest's web site.

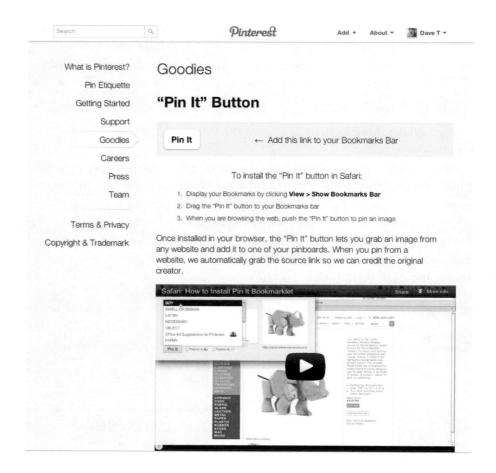

Start Pinning

Now that you have the Pin It tool and a few boards, it's time for the fun stuff! There are a number of ways to go about finding content for your boards, including perusing the Pinterest site for images and videos, pinning directly from web sites, or uploading your content from your computer.

Currently Pinterest displays your pins in the same order you upload them—and you cannot move pins around on a board. So the last thing you pin will be the first pin shown.

Find Content on Pinterest

There are several ways to find great content on Pinterest that you can repin to your own boards. At the very top of the site beneath the main logo, there are menu items that direct you to pages of interest, as shown here, and explained next.

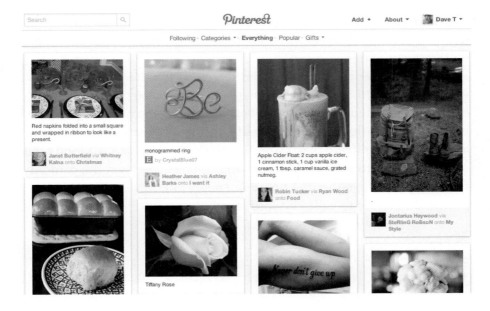

- **Categories**   This menu contains links to the most recent pins on the site organized into Pinterest's many categories (Art, Men's Fashion, Technology, Videos, and so forth). Hover your cursor over the link and select a category from the drop-down menu to view the most recent activity for that category. This can be a great way to find ideas for your own boards. For example, if you are planning a wedding and need a little inspiration, select Weddings from the menu to check out other pinners' ideas for venue choices, wardrobe, or even hairstyles.

- **Everything** The Everything page contains recent pins from all the categories on Pinterest. Click the Everything menu to get a glimpse of the latest pins on the site.

- **Popular** You can get a quick look at the most popular, recent pins on the site by clicking the Popular link. Popular pins are ones (from all categories) that have been repinned a number of times or have a large number of "likes" and comments from other users.

In addition to these three menus, there's another tool for you to use—the search box. If your interests don't fall neatly into the existing Pinterest categories, you can look for content from like-minded individuals by performing a keyword search on the site. For example, while there is a History category, there is no Genealogy category (an interest well-suited to Pinterest boards). You can type **genealogy** in the box at the upper-left corner of the site and click the search icon (it looks like a magnifying glass). The first thing that displays is a long feed of pins relating to your search term. You can narrow down the content further by clicking either the Board or People link to view boards or people that relate to your keyword search.

 You'll also see a drop-down menu labeled Gifts at the top of Pinterest, next to Popular. When you click Gifts, you get a selection of price ranges to choose from ($1–20, $30–50, and so forth). Selecting one of the ranges will return a new feed of pins of items for sale. For example, handmade or vintage items from the popular Etsy site or goods from big online retailers.

Repin Things You Find on Pinterest

As you've probably already discovered, some of the best content for your boards are things somebody else has already pinned. For example, if you are passionate about baking and happen across another pinner with a similar love of carbohydrates, you can repin their pin to your "I love baking" board. The repin you add will contain the original link (if there was one) as well as the image, as shown here.

cardamom mava cakes
•• by tartelette
31 likes 2 comments 61 repins

Any description that's already been added to the pin will automatically go along for the ride too, but you can type in your own description when you add it to your board; here's how:

1. Hover your mouse over the pin you want to repin. A Repin button will display.

2. Click the Repin button.

3. Click the arrow to display the drop-down menu for Boards and select one of your boards to pin the image to.

4. Highlight the existing text description (if it's not already highlighted) and add your own description of the pin.

5. Click the Pin It button to add it to your board. You can view the pin immediately or go back to the main page.

Include a description that will help you remember why you pinned the image and also why it's useful, interesting, or otherwise noteworthy. This also has the added benefit of helping other users by providing useful information about the source or purpose of the image that you're pinning.

Occasionally, pins from other users' boards have a bad link or don't contain the information you think they do. Before filling up your boards entirely with repins, check the link in the pin by clicking through to the image to make sure it has the information you're after.

Pin Web Content to a Board

After trawling through the far reaches of the Internet to discover the vintage car of your dreams or some other treasure, you can pin that content to the boards you've created.

To pin content from other web sites, do the following:

1. Locate an image that you want to pin on the site you're currently on.

2. Click Pin It in your browser's bookmarks bar; you'll be prompted to log into Pinterest, if you aren't already. All the pinnable images will display in your browser, as well as the dimensions of the image, as shown in Figure 2-3. You may have to scroll to find the specific image you had in mind.

3. Choose the image you want to pin by clicking it. The Create Pin window will display.

4. Select the board that you want to use from the drop-down menu and type a brief description of the pin.

5. Click Pin It.

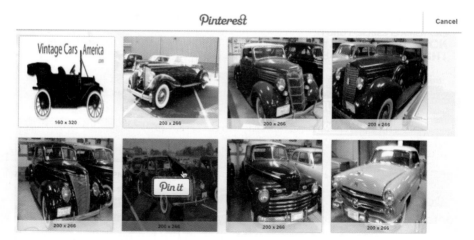

Figure 2-3   *Pin an image from a web site to one of your boards.*

The image dimensions are listed beneath the images after you click the Pin It button. If there are two versions of the same image, click the larger of the two to ensure you have the best-quality image on your board.

Pin Videos

If you find a video that you want to include on a board, such as a how-to video with home improvement advice, you can use the Pin It tool in your browser. From the page that contains the video, simply click Pin It, select the video (if there is more than one), and add it to one of your boards with a description.

Videos from sites like YouTube and Vimeo automatically cite the original source for the video when you pin them with the Pin It tool. For example, if you pin from YouTube, information about the video's creator will be added to your pin. If you pin a video from another web site, be sure to include information about the original source of the video to properly credit its creator.

YouTube has its own boards on Pinterest that you can pin freely from. Take a look at pinterest.com/YouTube. There are popular DIY, food, and style videos, as well as ubiquitous videos of cute animals.

Upload a Pin from Your Computer

If you have a collection of images on your computer, maybe some great shots of your travels or pictures of craft projects you've completed, you can share those on Pinterest as you would an image you find on the Internet. The difference between these types of pins is that they don't contain a link back to an original web site and have the words "uploaded by user" beneath the pin.

To add your own images to a Pinterest board:

1. Click Add at the top of the page.

2. Click Upload a Pin.

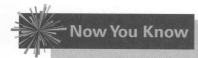

Now You Know   **Understand Types of Image Files**

Only certain image files can be uploaded to Pinterest, so you need to understand which image types to create in order to upload your images successfully. Pinterest supports JPEG and PNG images files only. You can see which type of file your image is by looking at the full file name on your computer. (If you cannot see the file extension, right-click for "full info" and look for file extension.) The file extension is .jpg for JPEGs and .png for PNGs. There is another commonly used file type (TIFF, with the extension .tiff), but this is not supported by Pinterest. You can easily change the type of image file you have by clicking the file name and adding the desired extension.

3. In the Upload a Pin dialog box that appears, shown here, click Choose File to locate the image file on your computer.

4. Choose a board from the drop-down menu, add a description, then click Pin It.

 **Now You Know**   **What If I Find a Great Pin that I Don't Have a Board For?**

If you happen across a pin that you want to add to Pinterest but don't yet have a board for it, you can create the board mid-pin (or repin, as the case may be). When you add a pin and you are in the editing screen, go to the bottom of the drop-down Boards list and select Create Board. Enter the name of your new board and click Create Board and the item you are pinning will be saved to the new board.

Delete a Pin from a Board

If you pinned the wrong image by accident or want to delete one for some other reason, you can accomplish this quickly on your Pinterest page. Find the pin you want to delete and complete the following steps.

1. Click your name on the main page to get to your page, then click the board that contains the pin you want to delete.

2. Point the cursor at that pin until you see the Edit button; click it.

3. Click Delete Pin in the Edit Pin screen. Confirm by clicking Delete Pin again when prompted.

Move a Pin from One Board to Another

You can move a misplaced pin from one board to another by working in the Edit Pin screen. To get there:

1. Click the pin you want to move.

2. Hover your cursor near the pin and click the Edit button when it appears.

3. Select a new board from the drop-down menu next to Board as shown here.

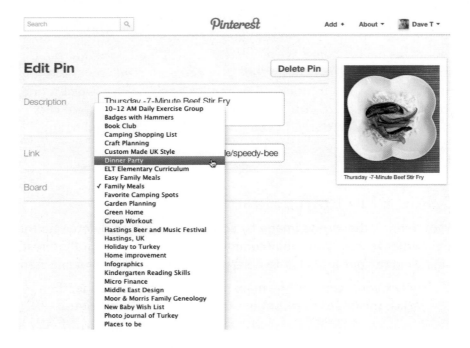

4. Click the Save Pin button.

3

Customize Your Pinterest Settings

You can control much of what displays on your Pinterest profile, including the frequency and the type of notifications you receive, what images display on your boards, and how your boards are arranged. Some of the suggestions we make in this chapter are intended to help you manage your privacy. Pinterest is a public site and anything you post, including personal information in your profile and the content of your boards, can be viewed by anyone. We'll look at how you can manage your pins, change your profile name and picture, add a web site and location, and control what is shown in social networks.

Customize Your Profile

As a member of the Pinterest community, you'll have a profile that displays to anyone browsing your boards. Your profile includes your full name, a picture, and a brief sentence or paragraph that you write about yourself or your interests. In addition, your profile picture is shown next to comments you make and things you repin. All of these items can be customized to show as much—or as little—about yourself as you care to.

Change Your Display Picture

If you initially signed up with your Facebook or Twitter account, then your profile will display the photo associated with that account by default. If you are comfortable including this on your public Pinterest profile, then you can skip to the next section. At present there is no such thing as a private profile on Pinterest. If you don't want to include a personal image, you can use a favorite photograph or one that embodies one of your interests—like a cleverly decorated craft project you've done or an item in one of your collections.

Keep in mind when you are looking for a suitable image that the dimensions of a Pinterest profile picture are square (160 × 160 pixels to be exact), but you can experiment with images to see which fits best in your profile. If you have a rectangular image, it will be cropped and centered to fit into your profile and you may lose some of the detail. If you have a very small picture, it will be stretched to fit and may appear distorted.

Once you've located an image on your computer that you want to use, do the following to add it to your profile:

1. Hover over your name in the upper-right corner and select Settings.

2. Scroll to the Image section and click Upload an Image (see Figure 3-1). You will also be given the option of refreshing your profile picture from your current Facebook or Twitter profile picture.

3. Click the Choose File button and locate the image file on your computer. Double-click the image to see a preview of it in your profile.

4. Click Save Profile at the bottom of the page.

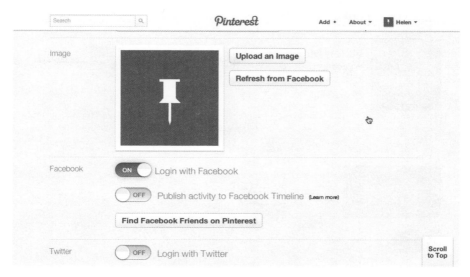

Figure 3-1 *Upload an image to display on your Pinterest profile.*

 The Refresh from Facebook (or Twitter) option will only appear if you still have one of the accounts linked to your Pinterest page. If you changed your image on one of these social sites and click the Refresh button, your most recent image will display on your Pinterest page.

Include an "About" Description

To further personalize your profile, you can include information about yourself or what you are interested in pinning. You don't need to be too personal—it can be something simple like "chocolate lover" or "antique map collector" or a list of all the things you are interested in pinning or other hobbies and pursuits.

   To add a brief description:

1. Click your user name in the upper-right corner.

2. Click the pen icon next to the words "write a little about yourself" and a small entry field will display as shown here:

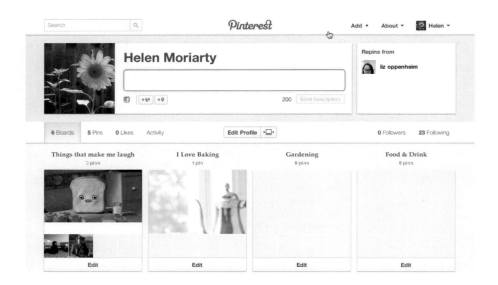

3. Type your description then click Save Description.

You can add things to your description or change it any time by clicking your user name and selecting Settings. Type over your existing description or alter it as you like.

Change Your User Name or Display Name

When you signed up for Pinterest, you entered your first and last name and created a user name for your page that becomes part of the address or URL that identifies your Pinterest boards. You can change both your user name and the name that displays on your page after you've set up your account if you decide to. For example, you may want to include only the first initial of your name to preserve some privacy or perhaps you'd prefer to include your nickname so that friends and family looking for you on the site can identify you more easily.

To change the names associated with your account:

1. Hover over your name in the upper-right corner and select Settings.

2. Scroll to the First Name and Last Name fields and edit your name.

3. In the Username field, enter a new user name. You may have to try more than one option if the name is already taken. If you create a new user name that is available, you'll see Available in green letters next to the Username field as shown here:

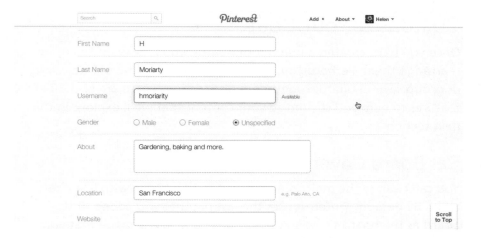

4. Scroll to the bottom of the page and click the Save Profile button.

 Beneath your name and user name you can opt to select Unspecified next to Gender if you prefer not to have that information publicly available or if you are using the account for an organization or business.

Add a Location or a Web Site

If you have a blog or web site that you want to share with other Pinterest users, you can add a link to your site on your Pinterest profile. If you are interested in connecting with people locally, you can choose to include your location on your profile as well.

To add your web site and location to your Pinterest profile:

1. Hover over your name in the upper-right corner and select Settings.

2. Scroll to the Website field and enter the URL for your web site.

3. Add your city, region or state in the Location field if you want.

4. Click the Save Profile button at the bottom of the page.

Customize Your Boards

Once you have created a number of boards, you may want to edit or rearrange them. Perhaps you want to change the name of one board, or group several boards together in one section. There are also other features to help you customize your content that we'll explore in this next section.

Set Board Covers

You can change the main image, or cover, of a board with just a few clicks. By default, Pinterest uses the last pin that you added to the board as the board's cover. You may have a favorite image that you want to show off, or maybe a funny or inspirational quote that you'd like others to see.

To set a board cover:

1. Click your user name in the upper-right corner.

2. Hover over the board cover you want to change and click the Edit Board Cover button when it appears.

Figure 3-2 *Select an image to use as a board cover.*

3. Scroll through the pins by clicking the right or left arrow on either side of the image as shown in Figure 3-2.

4. Position the image in the frame so that the section you want to display is in the center of the frame—this is what will display as your board cover.

5. Click Set Cover.

Edit a Board

You can change the name of your board, the description of a pin in the board, and other information. Maybe you want to improve on a description of a pin or perhaps you've thought up a better name for the board. Whatever your reasons, you can edit your boards at any time, as explained next.

 Keep in mind that changing the board's name will change the URL. If you've shared the link with someone, that link won't work anymore.

1. Hover over your user name and select Boards.
2. Locate the board you want to change and click Edit to bring up the Edit Board dialog box.

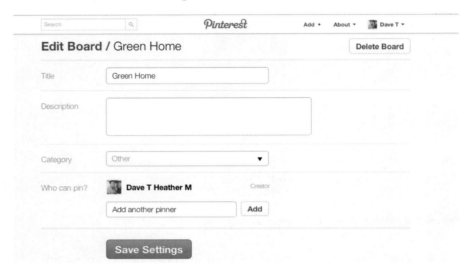

3. Enter a new name for the board.
4. Change or add a description.
5. Add or change a category by selecting one from the drop-down menu next to Category.
6. Click Save Settings.

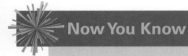 **Now You Know** **Categorize Your Boards**

If you don't add a category to a board, somebody else might. Pinterest encourages other users to help their fellow pinners add categories to their boards. If someone happens across your board and it's uncategorized, they can add a category. This is done to help other users find your content. You can change the category to one you select at any time. After you set the category, nobody else will be able to change it.

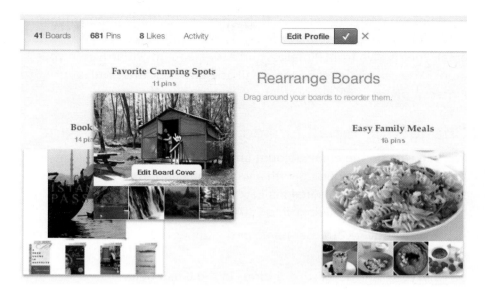

Figure 3-3 *Rearrange your boards in any order.*

Rearrange Boards

If you have a favorite board that you want to move to the top of your boards, or if you want to rearrange your boards in some other way, you can do this in a few simple steps on your main Pinterest page.

1. Click your user name in the upper-right corner to get to your main page.

2. Click the Rearrange Boards icon, shown here, which is next to Edit Profile.

3. Click and drag on a board to reposition it (see Figure 3-3). Repeat this for other boards you want to rearrange.

4. When you are finished, click the red check mark at the top of the page to save the arrangement.

Change Email Settings and Notifications

Once you are actively participating on the site, you may notice your email inbox filling up with notifications from Pinterest. By default, Pinterest will send you an email to let you know of any comments, likes, or repins your content receives. If you pin a particularly popular image, you can look forward to a dozen or more emails! You can control what email you receive from Pinterest and how frequently it arrives in your inbox. You can also change the email account associated with your Pinterest page—we'll show you how in this next section.

Change the Email Linked to Your Pinterest Page

You can change the email account linked to your Pinterest page at any time. Maybe you signed up with a work email address and need to switch over to your personal mail account.

To change the email linked to your page:

1. Hover over your user name in the upper-right corner and select Settings.

2. Type over the existing address in the Email field.

3. Scroll to the bottom and click the Save Profile button.

 Your email address is not shown on your page; it's only used to send you notifications about your content and for news and updates from Pinterest.

Set How You Receive Notifications

If you find Pinterest notifications cluttering up your inbox, you can change how often you receive notifications and select the types of notifications you want to receive. For example, you may not need to know every single time someone "likes" a pin of yours but you may enjoy reading comments from friends or followers on the site.

To control notifications:

1. Hover over your name in the upper-right corner and select Settings.

2. Click the Change Email Settings button.

3. Turn off the notifications you don't want to receive as shown in Figure 3-4 (Comments, Likes, Repins, Follows, and so forth).

Figure 3-4 *Control the notifications you receive from Pinterest.*

4. Choose how often you want to receive notifications by selecting the radio button next to Immediately or Once Daily.

5. Choose whether to receive news and digest emails from Pinterest by turning those options Off or On.

 There is an option to turn off notifications for Group pins. We'll explore how to create and manage group boards, including notifications, in Chapter 4.

Change Your Password

You should have a strong password for your Pinterest account. A strong password is one that contains a combination of letters, numbers, and symbols and is over eight characters long. It should also be different from the password you use for your email and other online accounts.

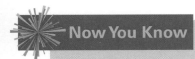

Now You Know | **Keep Your Account Safe**

In addition to protecting your account by using a strong password, here are two simple things you can do to ensure that your personal settings are secure and that the content you create is controlled only by you:

- Avoid using third-party apps that ask for your Pinterest user name and password.
- Don't share your user name and password with anyone else.

The only time you will be asked for your account information is when logging into the Pinterest site or using an official Pinterest app. Pinterest will never ask for your password by email, phone, or instant message.

To change your password:

1. Hover over your user name in the upper-right corner and select Settings.
2. Click the Change Password button.
3. Enter your old password in the first field.
4. Type in your new password and confirm it in the two fields following, then click the Change Password button.

Control What You Post on Social Networks

While all your content on Pinterest is public by default, there are some ways that you can limit how much exposure your Pinterest activity is getting by limiting where your activity is published on other social networks you have linked to Pinterest. You can also hide your boards from search engines if you choose. (On the other hand, if you are a designer or aspiring chef, or if you run a small business, you probably want all the attention you can get and won't want to do any of these things!) We'll show in this section how to control your content on social networks and hide your boards from search engines.

Remove Your Pinterest Activity from Facebook Timeline

If you have your Facebook account linked to Pinterest, your pins and activity will show up in your Facebook Timeline. You may like that your Facebook friends can see what you are up to on Pinterest but if you don't, you can change the setting and still opt to share the occasional pin on Facebook.

To disable publishing to your Facebook Timeline:

1. Hover over your name in the upper-right corner and select Settings.

2. Click the button next to "Publish Activity to Facebook Timeline" to select Off.

3. Click the Save Profile button to finish.

Control What You Share on Facebook and Twitter

If you want to share select pins with your Facebook friends or Twitter followers, you can do so when you are creating a pin, provided your Pinterest account is still linked to Facebook and/or Twitter. Simply select the check box next to Facebook and/or Twitter as shown in Figure 3-5.

Hide Your Content from Search Engines

You can hide your boards and profile from search engines if you are interested in limiting the number of people who will view your content.

Figure 3-5   *Share select pins on Facebook or Twitter.*

Pinterest boards and profiles regularly show up in search engine results—which is a good thing for many people (and businesses) who want to share their content with as broad an audience as possible. If you are not among them, here's how to hide your profile and boards:

1. Hover your cursor over your name in the upper-right corner and select Settings.

2. Scroll down to Visibility and change the setting to On to hide your profile and boards from search engines.

3. Click Save Profile at the bottom of the page.

Pinterest will add a tag to your content that tells search engines to ignore your page. Your information may remain in search results for a week or more while the change takes effect.

4

Become a Social Pinner

Pinterest is, above all else, a social sharing web site. While it's true that you might want to create boards with entirely your own content or boards that don't attempt to engage other Pinterest members (and we go into details of some of these in Part II of this book), this will probably constitute a small amount of your Pinterest activity.

At its core Pinterest seeks to connect people through the things they like. So in order to get the most out of the site, you will want to open yourself up to the idea of making these connections, and learn how to make them. You can then learn how to manage your connections, and how to contribute to the community.

In this chapter we will look at how to make new friends on Pinterest, how to manage those friendships, and how to see who is interested in your content. We'll also cover how to make contact with people you already know (whether they are on Pinterest or not) and how to involve them in your boards. In addition, we will look into the basics of how to interact with other people's content. This chapter should help to set you up with people to inspire you, get your friends engaged in Pinterest, and make you the ultimate social pinner.

Learn About Following

Those of you who already use Twitter will be very familiar with the concept of "following." For those of you who are not, to *follow* simply means to agree to view what someone posts. Unlike with Twitter, Pinterest allows you to follow all of a certain user's content, or just part by following a user's individual boards rather than the user. If you do choose to follow a person or board, all of the content that person pins (or is pinned to the board you follow) will appear on your main screen—the screen showing your activity you see when you are logged in at Pinterest .com whenever you visit the site (see the following illustration). The idea is that you choose to follow people who usually pin things you like, so you can enjoy their content and repin or comment on it. Another benefit is that other people's pins often give you ideas for original things to pin yourself.

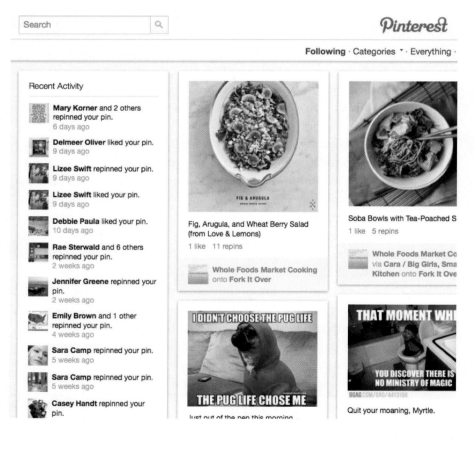

Find People and Boards to Follow

Finding people and boards to follow is one of the first steps to getting a steady flow of content that fits your particular interests into your Pinterest account. Of course, you will want to connect with your existing friends and we will cover that in the next section. However, there are definitely other types of pinners you should consider following in order to increase the variety of content flowing to your account. You could follow power pinners—these are people who engaged with Pinterest early on and have a consistent record of pinning great content.

A great way to find these people and see what types of things they pin is to hop over to the popular pinners section of Repinly (repinly. com/popular_pinners). This section of the site specializes in highlighting the most-followed pinners on Pinterest. You'll see a listing on the left of the page of the most popular pinners (determined by number of followers), and on the right you'll find recommendations of others to follow (see Figure 4-1). You can explore their content and choose to follow them directly from Repinly by clicking the user's profile picture or user name and then clicking Follow Me On Pinterest. You could alternatively make a note of the user names and find them on Pinterest using the search box (and setting the results to show only people).

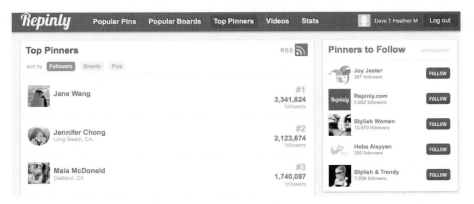

Figure 4-1 *Repinly's listings of popular pinners, showing most-followed pinners and recommendations of other pinners to follow*

When you find the pinners you want to follow, click their user name and you'll be taken to their boards page. You can choose to Follow All, which will flow all of their content into your main page, or click Follow under the individual board(s) you want to follow.

 When you start to follow a person or a board, you don't just get their new content, you also get all of their past content arranged chronologically.

You might also want to consider following companies and brands you like. Many name brands have Pinterest accounts, and use them to share new product lines, current promotions, and press releases. You can find companies and brands using the search box on Pinterest, but the search works on text matches only within the name and description fields. A better way to make sure you are following the official account of a brand or company is to visit their web site and look for the Follow Us On Pinterest button there. This illustration shows an example of where you might locate these "follow" buttons.

How to Unfollow

While finding someone to follow is easy, unfollowing (should you wish to) can be a little trickier. The most logical place to do this is from your main page, as this is where you are most likely to notice content you are not interested in. If you are following all of a user's pins and you wish to unfollow them, you simply find a pin from the user and click their user name there. This will take you to their boards page, where you simply click the Unfollow All button. This will remove them from your list. (The button will appear dimmed and when you click it, it will change to Follow All, in case you change your mind.)

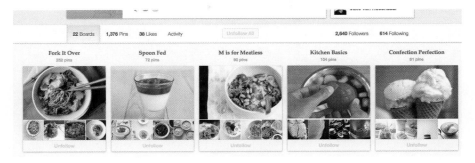

As described in Chapter 1, when you sign up for Pinterest, you are asked to choose interests that you have. Based on these choices, Pinterest will generate 25 boards you might like to follow and automatically set you as following them. This tends to place a lot of content on your main page that you might not want. In these cases you are mostly likely following only one board for each of these users, so you'll need to click the board name on one of the pins rather than the user name. You can then click the Unfollow button for that board.

Quickly See Followers and Following

If you are curious as to who is following you and whom you are following, you can find these details pretty quickly on your profile page. You may elect to have an email sent to you whenever you acquire a new follower (see Chapter 3 on how to do this), but it's hard to keep track. The same applies to those you are following. To see a list of people you are following and people that are following you, click your user name on the top right of any Pinterest page (next to Add and

About) to see your profile page. The bar above your boards shows you how many followers you have and how many you are following.

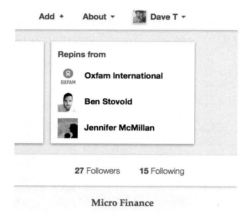

Click each number to take you to a detailed list of your followers or the pinners you are following. You can also check any pinner's profile page to see who is following them—this is a great way to find more fun people to follow.

Connecting with Friends

One thing you most certainly want to do is to connect with your existing friends and family so you can all enjoy each other's content. How to do this roughly breaks into two areas—connecting with those who are already registered with Pinterest and inviting people who are not registered. The Pinterest site makes both of these processes very easy, and always seeks to leverage your existing contacts before resorting to slower manual efforts.

Connect with Friends Registered on Pinterest

Connecting with friends already on Pinterest is very easy to do. Strangely, the site has a menu option of both finding people and inviting people, but they lead you to an identical page.

To navigate to this section of the site, simply click the arrow next to your user name on the top right of your Pinterest home page. You should then select the option Find Friends or Invite Friends. The page you arrive at will give you the option to invite or find people in four different ways—email, Facebook, Gmail, and Yahoo! mail. The first option, email, encourages you to invite friends by emailing them a link to join Pinterest. This should be left for last as you wouldn't want to invite people without first checking to see if they are existing Pinterest members.

To get started:

1. Click one of the three services listed on the right that you use (Facebook, Gmail, or Yahoo! mail)—we use all three so we went through this process service by service. If you are not logged into the service you clicked, Pinterest will ask you to do so on that page.

2. Once logged in, a pop-up will appear, generated by the service (not Pinterest) asking for your permission to allow Pinterest to access your contacts. If you wish to proceed, then you must agree—we have connected dozens of accounts in this way and have had no security or privacy issues resulting from this.

3. Once you allow, Pinterest will search through your contacts and divide them into two lists: those already registered with Pinterest and those who are not. The former will appear in a vertical list on the right side of the page.

4. Simply click the Follow button next to each name to connect with that person.

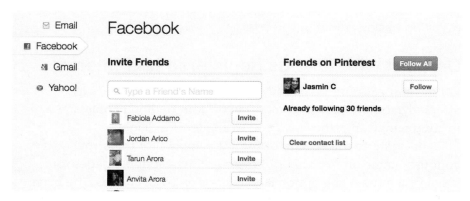

Invite Friends to Join Pinterest

If friends from your email contacts list are not registered, they will appear in a vertical column on the left. They will need to be invited to Pinterest, and you can do this by clicking Invite next to their names. If your list of friends is very long, you can filter it by using the search box—simply start typing someone's name and the list will be reduced to match what you typed. If you invite someone, you will see a pop-up giving you the option to add a message to the invitation. Because many people are suspicious of automated emails, you might like to include a personal note here so it won't look like spam. The invite will be sent to the person either by email or Facebook, depending on which service you chose to use.

Engaging with People's Content

Now that you have connected with the people you know, you will be able to see their pins and boards and interact with them. Interactions with pins break into three main areas—commenting, liking, and repinning (covered in Chapter 2).

Liking and Commenting on Pins

The first way to engage with a pin is pretty self-explanatory and likely very familiar to users of Facebook—this is to "like" a pin. To do this, you simply hover your cursor over the pin. You will see three buttons appear: Repin, Like, and Comment. To like the pin, simply click Like. The only thing you will see happen is the button then becomes dimmed and the text changes to Unlike. If you clicked Like by accident, simply click Unlike and your like will be removed. Depending on the original pinner's account setting, they may receive a notice saying you liked the pin. You will see the same thing happen when other pinners like your pins, if you have set up your account notifications for that.

If you wish, you can comment on any pin you see—in fact, you are encouraged to do so! To do this, hover over the pin and click Comment. A text box will appear under the pin with your profile picture next to it. You can type whatever you would like to say here, with a limit of 1000 characters (although users may not care for this length of comment as it makes the pin's on-screen footprint much larger). When you have finished typing, click the Comment button under the box you were typing in.

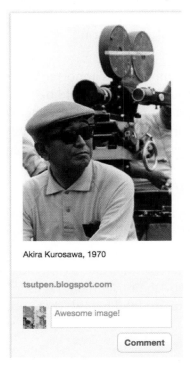

Akira Kurosawa, 1970

tsutpen.blogspot.com

Awesome image!

Comment

Now You Know   How to Report a Pin

If you feel a pin is offensive (as opposed to just not being to your taste), you can report it to Pinterest. To do this, click the pin image. You will arrive at a page with a much larger version of the pin. On the right of the image you will see five buttons, the fourth of which is Report Pin. If you click this button, you'll be asked why you wish to report it. The options Pinterest offers are:

- Nudity or pornography
- Attacks a group or individual
- Graphic violence
- Hateful speech or symbols
- Actively promotes self-harm
- Spam
- Other (choosing this will open a text box for you to explain)

These reasons for reporting a pin comply with Pinterest's user policies.

When you make a comment, it's important to follow the rules of Pinterest Etiquette. Your comment should be respectful, positive, and useful to other users, and not offensive or rude. You will doubtless see things you don't like on Pinterest, but you should avoid commenting on these. If you feel the pin is offensive, then you can report it.

Mention a Pin to Another User

When commenting on a pin, you have the option to bring the pin to another Pinterest user's attention. To do this, you first need to be following at least one board belonging to that user. When you are ready to mention the pin to the other user, type the @ symbol immediately followed by their user name. A list of potential matches to this user name will begin to load below where you are typing.

When you see the person you want, click their name. Once you submit the comment, the user you mentioned will receive a notification that you mentioned them.

It's also worth noting that, in addition to mentioning a user in a comment, you can mention them in a pin description while you're pinning or repinning.

Use Hashtags in a Pin

A hashtag is a way of tagging a pin with keywords. On Pinterest you can use hashtags in the description field of any pin, and you create them by using the # symbol directly before the word you wish to tag. For example, to tag a pin about the Oakland Athletics, we could use the tag #oaklandathletics. You need to avoid using spaces between words, as only the first word will be tagged. Once you submit the pin, the hashtag will become linked, so users can click it.

Users of Twitter will be very familiar with hashtags. However, it's important to note that Pinterest does not treat hashtags the same way as other social sites. On Twitter, for example, when you click a hashtag, you will be shown the most recent tweets that also contain that hashtag. On Pinterest, when a user clicks the linked hashtag, they will be shown all pins containing the word or phrase after the # symbol in their title or description, whether or not the word or phrase was tagged in those titles or descriptions.

Starting Group Activities on Pinterest

Now that you have your friends on Pinterest and have come to grips with the basics of pinning and commenting, you might start some group projects. One such idea is to create a group board—one that users you select and invite can collaborate on and pin to. Specific examples of this type of collaborative board are mentioned in Part III.

Create a Group Board

A group board allows multiple people to contribute to it (as opposed to the default setting of only the creator). The process of creating a group board is identical to creating a personal board (see Chapter 2) aside from the additional step of the creator declaring who else can pin to it.

To create a group board, click Add in the top right of your Pinterest main page. Select the option Create A Board. You should name and categorize your board as you would normally. You will then notice the third section of the create page—Who Can Pin? The creator is always included by default. If you wish to add another person, it must be a pinner whom you follow, or who follows you. To add them, type their Pinterest user name in the text box. As with mentioning someone in a pin, matching user names will start to appear below the text box. Simply click the user you wish to allow to pin to your board, and then click the Add button.

Edit Board / Middle East Design

Title	Middle East Design

Description	I love Middle Eastern design - geometry and natural features over deceptions of likenesses.

Category	Art ▾

Who can pin?	David Todd	Creator

H| Add

H Morris

Save Settings

Unfortunately, this system was previously gamed by spammers, who allowed all of the people they were following to pin to their boards. This caused that board to show up on many people's Pinterest main page without their knowing the owner or agreeing to contribute. To counter this, Pinterest made it mandatory for pinners to accept the invitation to contribute to another user's board. This means those you ask to contribute to your board must formally accept. When they log into Pinterest and visit their boards, they will see the invitation and option to contribute there (see Figure 4-2).

You have a new board invitation.

Middle East Design
11 pins

David Todd invited you to this board

Accept   No Thanks

Figure 4-2 *An example of the message you will see on your boards page when you are invited to contribute to someone else's board*

5

Use Mobile Apps and Third-Party Products

The biggest growth areas in Internet technology are social and mobile—the sheer volume of social sharing web sites and mobile apps is testament to this. Already being a social site, Pinterest has been very quick to move into the mobile arena with their own mobile apps. And if their mobile apps don't currently support the tablet or phone you use, there is also a mobile-optimized Pinterest web site you can use on your mobile device, so you are not entirely tied to Pinterest's development cycles for their stand-alone mobile apps. In addition to the mobile options Pinterest offers, third-party developers have been extremely active in building web applications that complement Pinterest.

In this chapter we will look at the Pinterest mobile options. We'll also look at some of the best (and most reliable) web applications that are around today—what they can do, what they can't do, and how you can use them. We'll cover applications that help you to understand what others are pinning, see how your pins are received, add sharing options to blogs, and make pins when you don't have an image.

 New apps come and go pretty quickly so what we will showcase here are those that have proven reliable over the last six months or so.

In terms of mobile apps, there are currently three available from Pinterest—the iPhone app, the iPad app, and the Android app (which works on both cell phones and tablets). However, a quick search in the Apple App Store and on Google Play (the primary store for Android apps) reveals there are dozens of third-party apps, largely from unknown publishers. Some are free and some are not. Given that these were not developed by Pinterest (or any other reputable developer), we will not be focusing on them in this chapter. This is not to say they are bad, but there is an element of risk in downloading these as some may contain malware or heavy advertising. If you are tempted by them, make sure to check out the user reviews first.

Using the Pinterest Mobile Applications

In addition to the official mobile suite of apps, Pinterest also has a mobile-optimized web site—m.pinterest.com, also sometimes called an "em-dot" site—which you can use to access your Pinterest account from a smartphone or tablet. One major benefit to using Pinterest on mobile devices is that you can browse content on the app or web site without logging in to your account—something most social sites do not allow. So people interested in Pinterest can have a good idea of what the site is about without being registered or having to download anything.

The apps themselves have some great functionality, but also some restrictions. For this reason, we will look at each offering by device and walk through what they offer you.

Using the Pinterest Mobile-Optimized Site

The mobile web site, m.pinterest.com, works on any smartphone and your browser will probably redirect you to this address when you type pinterest.com or click a search result for Pinterest. This site is somewhat limited, but allows you to see pins from those you follow on the home page once you are logged in. The site always opens to pins from people you follow; an example of this view is shown in Figure 5-1.

You can navigate to your boards by tapping your profile image at the top right of the page and selecting Profile. Figure 5-2 shows how your profile page appears if you choose the boards view, with your

Figure 5-1   *The default homepage on the Pinterest mobile web site*

follower/following details at the top and your boards shown tiled underneath. You can like, comment on, and repin any pins, and search

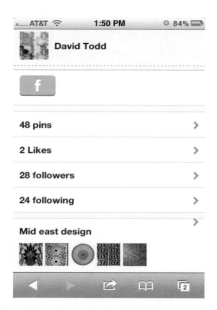

Figure 5-2   *The profile and boards section on the Pinterest mobile web site*

for things (using the magnifying glass icon at the top right of the page, as shown in Figure 5-1). The drawback is that if you don't use a downloadable app, you cannot pin directly from your mobile phone's web browser and you cannot directly pin photos you take with your phone's camera or photos you have in your images folder.

Using Pinterest on Your iPhone

If you have an iPhone, you have the choice to browse your Pinterest boards on the mobile-optimized web site or by using the iOS app—or for best results, use both. Using both allows you to overcome drawbacks to only using the mobile site mentioned in the previous section—namely not being able to pin without the downloadable app.

If you install the Pinterest app, available for free from the Apple App Store, you will be able to pin directly from the Web and pin photos you take with your iPhone—offering you *almost* the same functionality you have on your home computer. We say almost because you can't edit pins, boards, or change descriptions.

In order to pin directly from Safari, you will need to install the Pin It bookmarklet for iPhone—this is the equivalent of adding the Pin It button to your toolbar as described in Chapter 2. The process of adding this feature to Safari for iPhone is a little trickier than adding it to the toolbar on your computer because the mobile browser has no toolbar. The Pinterest help pages have a step-by-step tutorial on how to add the Pin It bookmarklet, which can be found at http://pinterest.com/iphone/bookmarklet/. The basic steps are

1. Create a bookmark.
2. Copy the Pin It bookmarklet code.
3. Edit the bookmark, pasting the bookmarklet code as the URL.
4. Save.

Once the Pin It bookmarklet is installed, you can pin from the Internet. When you see something you want to pin, open your bookmarks and select the Pin It bookmark. You will then see the images and videos that can be pinned from that page. Select the image or video to pin, you will then be switched from Safari to the Pinterest app to complete your pin.

Pinning photos you take using your iPhone camera is all managed seamlessly through the app itself. The menu row at the bottom of the app interface contains a camera icon; tapping this will launch your camera and you can snap away. If you want to pin from your photos folder or Camera Roll instead of taking a photo to pin, you can do this by tapping the camera icon and then tapping the double square icon at the bottom right of the screen as shown in Figure 5-3. Once you have taken a photo, you can use the app to adjust the brightness (by holding your finger on the image and dragging it across the screen), then tap the Use button and complete the pin details.

The app also allows you to explore pins by category, see pins from people you follow, repin images you find, delete pins, share pins via

Figure 5-3   *When the camera mode of the Pinterest mobile iOS app is open you use the camera icon to take a photo or the double square icon to select a photo from your Camera Roll or photos folder.*

Facebook, Twitter, and email, and check your recent news or activity, as shown in the illustration. You can access these functions by tapping the icons in the bottom row of the app on either side of the camera icon.

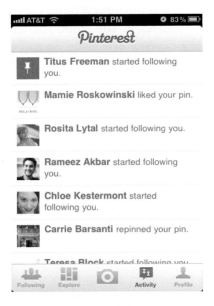

Using Pinterest with Your iPad

Using Pinterest on an iPad is a pretty slick experience. You can browse the full Pinterest site in your browser as you do on your computer—because Safari for iPad has a much larger screen than cell phones, you won't be redirected the mobile-optimized site. Alternatively, you can use the iPad app. Using Pinterest on the tablet's mobile browser (Safari) is the experience that gets closest to that of a standard computer—by adding the Pin It bookmarklet you can pin from the Web and do everything within Pinterest you would do on your computer. However, the Pinterest iPad app offers undeniably the most seamless self-contained mobile experience, allowing you to do away with switching between your preferred web browser and the iPad app or having to add Pin It bookmarklets.

If you prefer not to use the iPad app, you'll need to install the Pin It bookmarklet on your iPad's version of Safari. You can do this in two ways. The first way puts the Pin It button on your Safari toolbar on your iPad, which allows you to tap the button whenever you see something you wish to pin. Here's how:

1. First, add the Pin It bookmarklet to Safari in your *desktop computer's* toolbar. See the "Add the Pin It Button to Your Browser" section in Chapter 2.

2. Then go to System Preferences and select iCloud (or go to icloud.com).

3. Log into iCloud with your Apple ID and sync all your bookmarks from your desktop Safari to your iPad's Safari.

4. Sync your iPad with iTunes on your computer.

5. The Pin It bookmarklet will appear in your iPad Safari's toolbar, as shown in the following illustration.

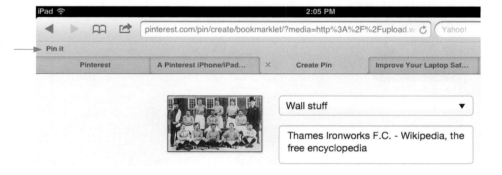

Now you can pin as you would on your computer, tapping the Pin It bookmarklet in your toolbar when you want to pin. While you can sync bookmarks between other browsers, notably Google Chrome, you can't launch them via the mobile version of the browser in quite the same way. There is a workaround for Chrome, but it's very complicated and clearly Safari makes pinning much simpler and more convenient.

The second way to pin directly from the Web on an iPad is to add the Pin It bookmark in exactly the same way you do for an iPhone (see "Using Pinterest with Your iPhone" for instructions on how to do this).

You have the option of adding it your toolbar (which will place it in exactly the same place as when you sync with iCloud) or adding it to your regular bookmarks list. If you choose the latter, you pin by tapping the bookmarks icon (open book) and selecting Pin It as shown in the illustration. You'll then see which items you can pin. You choose one and follow the instructions to complete the pin.

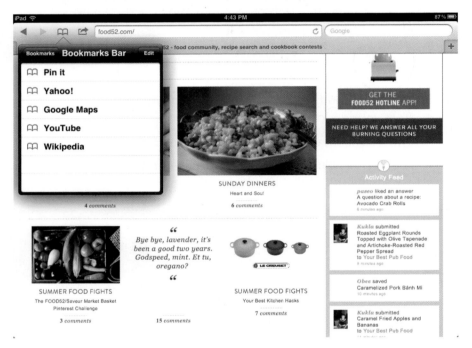

 The iPad copy and paste functionality sometimes strips an important piece of code from the bookmarklet meaning the button fails. You can find more reliable code here: http://heresthethingblog.com/2012/03/19/add-pin-button-ipad/.

While using Safari to pin from an iPad requires some set up, using the iPad app is a dream! Most of what the iPad app offers is similar to that of the iPhone app—you can browse your activity, repin, like, and comment. However, the big benefit is that the app has a built-in browser of its own, meaning there is no need to install any buttons at all.

To launch the built-in web browser, simply tap the menu icon (three horizontal lines) at the top left of the screen and tap Browse the Web. Enter the web site you wish to visit in the browser bar and tap the Go key on the keyboard. When you are ready to pin, tap the Pin It button next to the browser bar and you'll see what you can pin, as shown in the illustration. You are then able to complete your pin in the same way you do on a computer.

For all of this wonderful functionality, there are two downsides to the iPad app. First, there is no option to pin photos from your tablet (either using the camera or using images you have in your photos folder)—this means you are restricted to pinning things already on the Web, rather than being able to add things you see when out and about. The second downside is that the built-in browser doesn't have any bookmarking capability and has no built-in search box. The lack of bookmarking means you need to manually enter your favorite web sites each time you visit them, which is frustrating. The absence of a search box means you need to navigate to a search page to search for something; it's not a big deal, but it is an added step.

Using Pinterest on Android Devices

The Pinterest app for Android has one distinct advantage over its iPhone and iPad equivalents—it works on tablets as well as cell phones. This means you won't have to wait around for a tablet-specific version to be developed or have to use the smaller cell phone version on a larger tablet (which can be somewhat jarring).

The app itself offers pretty much the same as the iOS mobile apps. You can browse your pins and boards, check the activity of those you follow, and comment, like, and repin. It also allows you to create a pin from the images you have on your device or an image you wish to take—you can do this from the activity section of the app, which is the default entry point.

You'll find the Create Pin option at the top left of the screen; tapping this will give you the option to take a photo or choose one from your device. The Take Photo option will open the camera application, and the Choose Photo option will open your photos folder. Sadly, the app does not facilitate any pinning from the Web, so we are stuck with the Chrome hack mentioned in the following section.

Using Pinterest with Mobile Web Browsers

Pinning through a mobile browser other than Safari is technically possible—notably on devices equipped with Chrome. Unfortunately, pinning from Chrome is very tricky as you can only do it by pasting the Pin It bookmarklet code on top of the URL in the address bar when you are on a page that contains an image you want to pin. We are hopeful that other browsers will be better supported soon, but the development process for browsers is more complex than for apps. On iOS devices, the default browser is Safari and we'll focus on using that in this section. We'll also look at Yahoo! Axis, a new iOS browser app that has some excellent Pinterest functionality built in.

Pinning Through Safari (iPhone or iPad with Pinterest App Only)

We recommend following the instructions in "Using Pinterest on Your iPhone" or "Using Pinterest with Your iPad" for getting the Pinterest Pin It bookmarklet on your device. Once installed, you can use the bookmarklet in more or less the same way you use the Pin It button on your computer. Here's how:

1. Navigate to a page you want to pin from.

2. Open the bookmarks and tap your Pin It bookmark (or tap the Pin It button on your iPad Safari toolbar if you synced with iCloud).

3. Tap the image or video you wish to pin.

4. iPhone users will be switched to the Pinterest iPhone app to determine where you want to place that image. iPad users will complete their pin within Safari.

Although this seems complicated and perhaps a little confusing, this is a really good option for those of you who want to use Safari and keep your existing bookmarks, history, and search engine preferences, rather than starting from the blank browser canvas that the Pinterest app gives you.

Axis: Easy Browser Pinning (iPhone and iPad Only)

Yahoo! Axis calls itself the visual browser. It has a built-in search layer (using Yahoo! search only) and shows small page snapshots for the URL returned for your queries. It was released in May and has very favorable reviews in the Apple App Store in both iPhone and iPad forms.

The great thing about Axis for Pinterest users is that it comes with a Pin It button already installed. When you search, you can scroll through the matching web site snapshots and tap the one you want to view—this will open that page. If you want to pin from this page, you need to tap the Share button at the bottom (an arrow jumping out of a box), then tap the Pin It button from the menu that pops up (see the illustration). Choose the image you wish to pin and you'll be switched to whichever iOS Pinterest app you have installed to complete your pin.

Useful Third-Party Web Applications

Moving away from mobile phones and tablets and back to the computer, there are plenty of web applications that are geared towards adding functionality that Pinterest currently does not have. In this section we look at some tried and tested web apps that can be used to pin non-image items, sites that can provide you with statistics about Pinterest (including your own boards), and a couple of sites that offer great tie-ins to other sites. Finally, we'll look at some plug-ins and extensions for your desktop browser that can add some fun Pinterest functionality for you.

Making Pins from Non-images

When we create boards, we often come across the issue of how to pin things that are not images. Typically, these are things like events, locations, web sites, and simple text. Sometimes you can choose a substitute image and use the description to explain the pin, other times you can take screenshots and upload those. But this can be a hassle, and there are now some web sites that can turn the information you want to share into an image.

Pinstamatic (Pinstamatic.com)

This is by far our favorite supplementary Pinterest site! Pinstamatic helps you to get more from Pinterest by giving you the option to create a pin when you don't have an image for it. It allows you to create pins for locations, music track links (to Spotify), quotes, calendar dates, Twitter profile links, sticky notes, and web sites. For example, if you want to turn your favorite quote into a pin, you can do that using Pinstamatic.

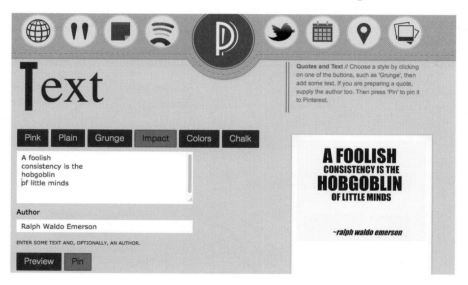

To use the site, hover your mouse cursor over each icon at the top of the page. A small label will appear telling what type of content each feature allows you to pin—hovering over the globe icon tells you that this is to pin web sites, for example. Simply click the icon at the top of the page that reflects the type of content you wish to pin and follow the instructions on that page to continue with your pin.

Depending on the type of content you want to create a pin for, these instructions will vary—for example, if you want to pin a music track, you only need to provide Pinstamatic the artist and track name and they'll generate the pin for you; if you wish to pin a quote, you'll need to provide the text and choose a style. Whichever content type you choose, your final option is always to go ahead and pin your content to Pinterest on the board of your choice.

Pinvolve

Pinvolve is an app that can be found on Facebook. It allows you to turn a Facebook page for which you are an admin into a pin board, making each post to that page a pinnable item. By Facebook page, we mean a subpage created within your own account to showcase a local event, company, brand, and so on (you can create pages by going to https://www.facebook.com/pages/create.php and selecting the type of page you want to set up)—not your own Facebook news feed or timeline.

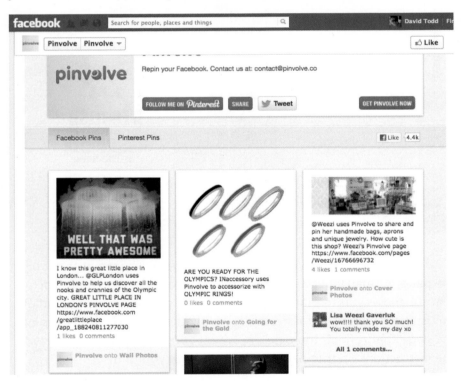

If you are logged in and an admin for the page you wish to transform, you can install the app. To install the app, enter **Pinvolve** in the search bar at the top of your Facebook homepage. Click the app when you see it appear in the search results. Then click Add to My Page, which will produce a pop-up menu asking to choose which of your pages you wish to enable Pinvolve on, and instructions to accept the terms and conditions.

Pinvolve then creates a new tab on your Facebook page that shows all of your image posts on a Pinterest-style pin board, complete with comments and likes that were made on Facebook. Clicking any Pinvolve picture will take you to the Facebook post for that image, but hovering will allow you to pin that image to Pinterest.

Shareasimage (Shareasimage.com)

Shareasimage is a great little bookmarklet that lets you turn any text you find on the Internet into a colorful pin. It is quicker and easier than Pinstamatic in that you don't need to copy and paste any text—you can simply highlight the text you want to turn into a pin and create the pin right from the web site. The downside is that Pinstamatic offers you more variety in the design of the pin, and adding color, background, and different fonts on Shareasimage requires a paid upgrade to their pro account. For these reasons, you should decide on your requirements before you choose which service to use.

You can install the bookmarklet on all major browsers. To install the free version, go to the Shareasimage.com web site, click the Try the FREE Version link, and simply drag the button onto your toolbar or bookmarks folder. To make a pin, highlight text on any web site and click the bookmarklet button. You will see your text converted to an image that is ready to pin and the image-editing options (locked on the free edition). You can then edit as you wish and pin!

Getting Pinterest Stats and Analytics

Understanding how people are engaging with your content and what people find interesting in general can be fun for any user to know. But for anyone using Pinterest to promote a brand or company, it's absolutely crucial. Whether you fall into the former category or the latter, there are already two very strong sites that can help you out with tracking your activity and understanding what is popular in the Pinterest community.

Pinerly (Pinerly.com)

Pinerly is a site designed to help both businesses and individuals market their content and track its performance. The service allows you to build a marketing campaign on Pinterest, suggests new content ideas, and tracks your campaign performance with a neat dashboard of easily accessible metrics.

While the site is very popular and very intuitive with easy-to-use menus and walkthroughs, you can't just dive in and use it right away. Pinerly initially places you on a waiting list, and you can gradually move higher up the list by getting friends to sign up. After you reach ten friends, it gradually unlocks its services. Once in, however, the step-by-step approach to developing your campaign and easily accessible dashboard make running campaigns really simple.

Repinly (Repinly.com)

As mentioned in the previous chapter, Repinly is a fantastic site that gives you an instant idea of what is popular on Pinterest. The home page will show you trending pins, popular boards within certain categories, popular pinners, and the most popular categories for people to pin in. Additionally, through the top menu, you can explore each of these things in greater detail.

This site can be really useful for a number of reasons. First, someone new to Pinterest can get a really strong idea of what the site is about and what the community likes. This can help you get started with successful pin boards. Second, you can register your own Pinterest site with this service and see how your pins are doing relative to others— the site computes your Pinterest score based on popularity, activity, and influence on Pinterest.

The third way this site can be useful is for people seeking to market to the Pinterest community. By exploring the stats available within the site, you can assess how best to market what you have and whether Pinterest is the right place for you, and understand what it takes to build a following there.

The Best of the Rest

Of course some sites don't fit into any of the categories we've described. So here we briefly cover a couple of the other favorites that can help you bring content into your Pinterest boards.

Polyvore (Polyvore.com)

A very popular category on Pinterest is women's fashion—making up around 7 percent of total pins according to Repinly. Among the most popular pins within women's fashion, a substantial number are from Polyvore. Polyvore is a fashion social-commerce web site that allows users to assemble sets of clothing from the web site's database of items. Because the site's database contains clothing from many different sellers, you can create an entire outfit in a unique way, taking shoes from H&M, pants from Gap, and so on. Once your outfit is created, there is a Pin It button to post an image of the entire ensemble to Pinterest. These pins are very engaging because you see everything all on one pin rather than individual items being spread out over a board.

Anything looks good with a missoni scarf

19 likes   81 repins

heather-morris-
1.polyvore.com

Pinstagram (Pinstagram.co)

We are big fans of Instagram—the mobile app that allows you to take photos, apply digital filters, and then share the images on a variety of social sites. What's fun about Instagram is that it creates square images (like the old Polaroid and Instamatic cameras) with a range of filters that can give your photos a nostalgic retro feel. The downside to Instagram is that it currently doesn't support sharing to Pinterest— enter Pinstagram. Through its web interface, the site allows you to pin any of your Instagram photos directly to Pinterest once you have connected your account.

Wordpress Sharing (Wordpress.org)

Wordpress is one of the most popular sites on the Internet. According to Alexa (a leading supplier of web site traffic data), Wordpress manages 22 percent of new web sites on the Internet. If you have a blog on Wordpress and would like to integrate a Pin It button for your post, then there is an easy way to do that. In addition to placing a Pin It button at the end of each post (as shown in the next illustration), the plug-in also allows you to determine what exactly gets pinned when someone clicks that button. Of course, pinners can always overwrite what you set, but many probably will not.

Now You Know   **Adding Pinterest Sharing on Wordpress**

Setting up the sharing option will take you five minutes:

1. Login to your Wordpress blog and navigate to the admin area.

2. Click on the Settings tab, then select Sharing.

3. Under the Sharing Buttons menu, drag the Pinterest (or any other) button from available services to enabled services.

4. Adjust any of the sharing options as you wish.

5. Save.

Bazaart iPad App (Bazaart.me)

One thing we would really like to get from Pinterest is the ability to move pins around on a board, so we can order them logically or stylistically. Sadly, this is not possible yet. However, something that's moving in that direction is the Bazaart iPad app, which allows you to make a collage of all of the images on someone's (anyone's) board and turn them into one pin. Once you have downloaded the app you can search for any Pinterest member by user name. The app will show you their pins—you can choose a board or select individual pins you would like to restyle. Simply tap each pin to add it to your collage, then tap Restyle. All of the images are placed onto a canvas. From here you can move the images around, resize them, rotate them, delete the ones you don't want, and move to the front or place them behind other images. Once you are done, tap Publish and it will create a single pin for you! It's lots of fun, but pretty addictive too!

Browser Extensions, Plug-ins, and Add-ons

Extensions, plug-ins, or add-ons are small downloads for desktop web browsers that allow your browser to do things it can't ordinarily do. For example, we use an add-on that allows us to take screenshots using our mouse's right-click menu option—this saves having to switch to a keyboard. There are many different such extensions out there relating to Pinterest that are very useful.

 Extensions, plug-ins, and add-ons are generally built to work not just with a particular browser, but also for a *specific browser version*. This means that if you use Internet Explorer version 9, you cannot use extensions developed for Firefox or Chrome, etc. You also may not be able to use extensions developed for Internet Explorer version 10.

We are big fans of Chrome and Firefox as these work fastest for us and seem less prone to bugs and malware. These two browsers also have what we would consider the best browser extensions. Here are some favorites.

Chrome Extensions

- **Pinterest Pro**   This extension allows you to do lots of handy Pinterest things very quickly. You can right-click any image on any web site and click Pin to Pinterest to instantly pin from the Web. You can view a larger version of any pin on Pinterest by hovering over it—so no need to click through. You can also see a random list of popular pins by clicking the Pinterest icon in your toolbar.

- **ShotPin**   This extension allows you to take a screenshot of any web page, then share it on Pinterest. This makes it very easy to pin a particular page you like, rather than just pinning an image or video.

Firefox Add-ons

- **Pinterest Right-Click**   This add-on allows you to choose the image you want to pin by right-clicking it rather than having to select it from all of the other pinnable content as you have to when using the Pin It button.

Part II
Explore Individual Project Ideas

Red walls!?

housepaintingtutorials.com

Design Tips for Small Bedrooms

2 likes 2 repins

sunset.com

Elipse chair. Not sure this would work with what we've got but it's funky.

insidemodern.com

Comfy looking poufs

1 repin

americangypsyliving.com

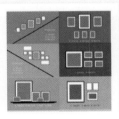

6

Building Boards for People and Places

So, you've jumped through the hoops Pinterest has asked you to jump through. You've registered, linked your Twitter or Facebook account if you wished to, added some friends, written something short about yourself, and uploaded a photo for your profile. Now comes the fun stuff!

From our experience across new social media (and any kind of web application really), it'll take you a little while to fully acquaint yourself with the product. You will probably be aware of the basic potential from just looking at the site. Indeed, your own ideas of what you want to do on Pinterest are probably your main motivation for registering. But it's wise (and fun) to just noodle around with the site and get to know it.

 The Pinterest site is in active development and the developers are continually making fixes and enhancements. You will notice the changes either through using the site or via an update on your Pinterest homepage and in your email. In the case of the mobile apps, you will be informed that a newer version is available and you can make the update as per your device specifications.

Throughout this chapter, we will focus on individual project ideas. These are defined as things you might typically do for your own benefit or appreciation (as opposed to things you might want to do for an intended audience). Within each board type, we chose one interpretation of that project and provide an example board for that. We also offer some general tips and advice about how you might like to go about building a board of this type. Of course, everyone is different and everyone's idea of a board is unique. What we offer are tips and suggestions that apply to the general theme. It is our hope that you might use these ideas to get yourself started as you begin your journey towards making the perfect board. Some people will say there is no such thing as a perfect board, but we would disagree. The perfect board is the one that does what you want it to. It may be fictional or frivolous, but it's designed by you and for you. If it works for you, then it has done its job.

Self-Pinterest: Use Pinterest's Starter Ideas

The self-interest board is a great one to start your Pinterest journey on because it will be wide open with possibilities and free from any expectations on your side.

You might be all ready to go on your first board, inspired by what you have already seen on Pinterest. If you are looking for inspiration, check out a great site—Repinly.com. Repinly keeps track of the most popular pins, repins, and boards on Pinterest on a category level as shown in Figure 6-1. You can quickly see what other people have done, what other people have liked, and draw some inspiration from there.

 See Chapter 5 for more information on Repinly.

As you can see, in the U.S. around 15 percent of pins are related to food. You can also see that the most popular boards are related to home décor. However, the most popular boards are not tied to one of the categories suggested by Pinterest. This might be because people are not always pinning with a focused area of interest—they are generally pinning things that interest them. You can click any pin or board you like on Repinly and it'll click through to Pinterest. From there you can explore the pinner and board more closely. You can also start your first board by repinning.

For both of us, the general pin board was our first foray into Pinterest. It's so easy and so much fun. If, like us, you spend a lot of time

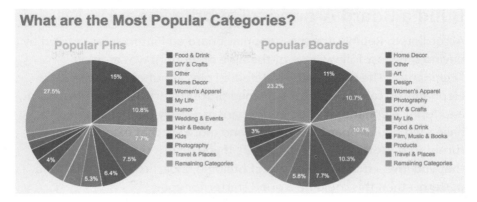

Figure 6-1 *A breakdown of the most popular pin and board categories as reported by Repinly*

on the Internet in general, you probably see lots of things you think are neat. Many times when we see these things we share them via social media so others can enjoy and comment on them. One of the downsides of sharing is that you cannot easily collect these things in one place and searching for them on your Facebook timeline, for example, or Sent email folder can be very difficult. This is where Pinterest can work well for you because it allows you to dedicate a space to whatever you want.

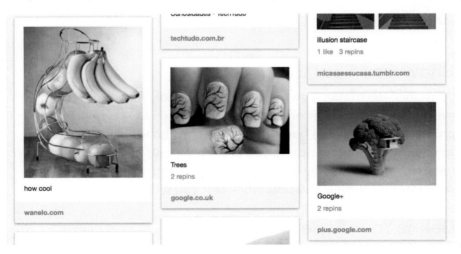

If you want to dive right in and start your first board, here are some ideas that we have enjoyed on the self-interest theme. These represent both boards we have made and others we follow and enjoy looking at.

Build a Board Around a Favorite Theme

According to Repinly, the most popular board on Pinterest (as defined by having the most followers as of the time of writing) was entitled "Elephants." The board simply contained pins about elephants— elephants on fabrics, elephant-themed products, articles about elephants, and funny elephant pictures. Your board can really be that simple. We have seen similar boards on giraffes and monkeys that extend to home furnishings, clothing, even nail polish. If you have a theme in your life that you love—it could be a type of building, a particular material, or a pattern—then this could be a good starter for you.

Just some of the dozens of tiles we lugged back from Iznik.

David Todd from

Another photolithograph we recently got.

David Todd from

Our Iznik tiles which we really need to do something with.

David Todd from

Showcase Cool Gadgets

Consumer electronics is an industry that is rapidly growing. Seemingly every week new devices are being unveiled and new capabilities being promised. This makes a good starter Pinterest board because if it's something you follow closely, you probably won't have to do too much research. You can simply visit all of the sites you usually visit in your daily Internet surfing and post whenever you see something you like.

Define Your Style

A style board is a Pinterest board used for pinning images that reflect a certain style you're trying to capture, very often with fashion or design. Sometimes you are searching for a wardrobe for a particular occasion—and using a Pinterest board for that is great. A lot of the time we see clothes we'd like, but are not really focused on buying them or may not even have an occasion to wear them. Pinterest can be great for collecting these ideas until the time comes to buy. It's also worth looking at a site called Polyvore.com. This site allows you to put together a style collage complete with accessories that you can then pin to your board. It only caters to women's wardrobes right now, however.

from Mad Men Collection at Banana
Republic

nymag.com

summer cool, created by
davetandheatherm on Polyvore

davetandheatherm.polyvore.c
om

Cute.

Build a Board Around a Design Theme

A design theme can be seen as taking some central theme and applying it to a design context. We see these boards largely dedicated to home design, but they don't have to be that focused or even that practical. You can see lots of examples of boards dedicated to individual shapes that contain art, food, products, architecture, and design ideas all around that theme. You can also find boards that are dedicated to certain cultural themes, like African design, Middle Eastern design, art deco design, and so on. There are boards dedicated to stones or shells as a design theme—the list is endless.

Focus on a Type of Food

Do you have a favorite food? This would make a great board to start off with. There are a great many examples of these on Pinterest dedicated to just about every type of food. These types of boards are generally made up of recipe pins, but you can also pin gadgets designed for that food, articles about growing or buying that food, and even products themed on the food.

Pin What You Find Funny

This is a personal favorite of ours, and a great candidate for first-time pinners. The category is also limitless in terms of what you might like to pin! If you have a favorite TV show, you can pin clips or images from that. You might also like to pin images that you find amusing—there are lots of pins of cute animals with captions (from sites like lolcats) and the inspirational posters with humorous captions. Some particularly creative boards we have seen are dedicated to amusing signage and terrible advertising campaigns.

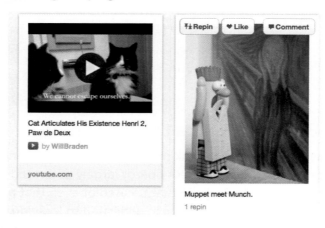

Cat Articulates His Existence Henri 2, Paw de Deux

by WillBraden

youtube.com

Muppet meet Munch.

1 repin

Round Up Places You Want to Go

Again, this is a very popular type of board with people creating their "someday" boards by the thousands. A great way to start this board is to think of all those places you have always wanted to go and pin images and videos of them. You can also pin things as you see them on the Internet as part of your daily browsing. There tends to be a lot of repins around places—this would seem to indicate Pinterest is a great inspiration source for would-be world travelers.

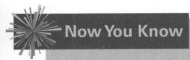

Get Good Content Sent to Your Email Inbox

If you are struggling to find good sources, you can try using an RSS feed to deliver good content to your email inbox. RSS feeds are mechanisms used by web sites to send regularly updated content (like articles and images) directly to people who subscribe to that RSS feed. When you are on a favorite web site, you can check to see if it has RSS feeds—virtually all of the most popular web sites do. Using a news search engine like Yahoo! or Google allows you to customize a news search that will send articles containing certain key words to your inbox. You can then click the articles and pin if you like something.

Pin People You Admire

Although most boards are dedicated to *things*, there are also plenty of boards about people. You can create a board of your heroes—people who inspire you. You can pin videos of memorable moments or classic images. You could even dedicate a board to just one person. One board that was great fun to create was our World Soccer XI board—it gave us a chance to read up on stats and build our own team rather than read other people's ideas. That approach could easily be applied to your favorite football or baseball team. You could build a board around actors or singers that you like, explaining in the description what you like about them or any favorite works they have produced.

Plan a Trip

Making a board to plan a trip is incredibly fun to do. You may not actually be anywhere near making the vacation real, but a lot of Pinterest boards are in the "someday" spirit as mentioned earlier in the chapter. The sample board we put together was for a dream vacation to Turkey we'd like to take. The act of creating the board gave us a greater sense of what exactly would be involved in making this trip in terms of costs and time. It also made us firm up a long list of ideas into what was actually achievable, which meant deciding what was really important to us on the vacation.

The most obvious thing to pin to a travel board is the sights you want to see—and we've included a section specifically on that. However, if the purpose of your board is serious planning (and not day-dreaming), then there are many other things you can add to your board to truly cover many of the areas that often occur as after-thoughts, causing you unnecessary stress later on. For us, one of the joys of this board was having a centralized place where we could store everything we needed to think about.

Research Destination Information

We found it helpful to dedicate a few pins to the actual destination in a very general way. Pinning general country information makes it easy to check back on little details like airports, major cities, transport links, and other things that we didn't pin specifically. On our board we went to the CIA World Factbook page for Turkey and pinned an image of the map. Although this pin does not display the actual information wanted, it allows us to get back to that page easily if we need to. You might also like to pin a map of your journey to your board. If you are thinking of a planned tour, then you can often pick up an image of the route from the tour operator's web site. For international travel, many of us like to

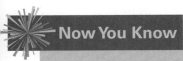

Now You Know **Add a Map to Your Board**

Map sites (like Google Maps in particular) will allow you to build a custom route map and save it. You can draw your route directly onto the map. You can add markers for sights, places to stay, and places to eat. You will need to register for this service, but the service is free and gives you a web URL you can use on Pinterest. Unfortunately, you will not be able to pin the map itself directly because it is not the type of image supported by Pinterest boards, but you can take a screenshot and upload that image from your computer.

learn a few key phrases in the local language. If so, you might also want to pin something related to local language—videos are fantastic for this and seeing them on your board reminds you to watch them!

Knowing what kind of weather to expect is essential for any trip as it affects how you might travel, what you will pack, and what you will be able to see. Finding the typical weather for a particular destination at a certain time of the year is very easy on the Internet, so you want to find a good site and pin from there.

If you are going to be dealing with a new currency, then Pinterest can be very useful. You can use your board to pin images of coins and banknotes and make notes about general conversion rates. This will help you get used to visualizing the money and remembering its value.

Think About Travel Safety and Requirements

If you are planning international travel then there are several important things you need to think about with regard to travel safety. We found things like visa requirements, government travel advisories, and recommended vaccinations very useful pins to have on the board because they are details that are often forgotten or left to the last minute and we wanted to have everything we needed to think about right there in front of us. Of course, making sure the country you are visiting is safe for tourism is a great idea. If you are planning to use a tour operator, then they should be considering this for you. But if you plan to organize your own trip, it's good to frequently check government-issued travel advisories.

For our board we went to the U. S. Department of State web site and pinned the only image available on the site—this was not ideal, but we really just wanted to bookmark the site, so it serves its purpose. You may also have to purchase a visa at some point. Even if you have a tour operator, visas are often not part of the service they provide, so it's a good idea to be aware of visa requirements, cost, and acquisition procedures. Some government sites will also tell you how you need to pay, so you can plan to have the right denominations of the right currency with you when you arrive. You will probably find that there is an English-language government/ministry site for the country you are visiting that you can pin from.

Depending on where you plan to travel and when, you may need to get up to date on your shot and vaccinations schedule, or even get covered for rarer local diseases. Check out your government or healthcare provider web site for this info and pin something from there. The Centers for Disease Control and Prevention is a great resource for this.

Consider Things You Need to Buy

There are always plenty of things to buy before a trip and we found it helpful to pin these items to the board. Pins of clothing are very useful because they can serve a number of purposes—you might need something special for a particular activity (like climbing shoes) or a climate that's different from where you live. For the Turkey vacation, we realized that we would need to have clothes that were suitable for hot weather but also modest enough to allow entry into religious buildings.

Aside from clothes, we also looked at durable suitcases that would suit a long tour, guidebooks we wanted to buy, and no-leak wash bags. You will certainly find many other things!

Plan Places to Visit

Pinning places to visit will likely be a big part of your board. Having great images on your board will make it look great, but we found it useful to be selective about where you are pinning from. Pinning directly from official sites will give you handy access to key details most reliably retrieved from official sources. While user-generated content (like that found on TripAdvisor) and local listings (like those found on Yelp) are great for leveraging reviews and personal experiences, they are notoriously unreliable for keeping accurate details of opening hours, ticket prices, and seasonal schedules. If you are planning to take your board with you (via the mobile Pinterest apps or a cell phone with Internet capability) then reference sites (like Wikipedia) are great sites to pin from as you can navigate the actual web page when you are in the location. Pinning from travel sites (like Lonely Planet) will also give you quick access to the must-see sections of the places you are visiting.

Shop for Souvenirs

When it comes to buying gifts for friends and relatives, we have spent many hours debating what to get for that difficult family member and what we can get (affordably) for groups of work colleagues. It's very hard on the spot when you have limited time and no access to buying guides. With this in mind, it's a nice idea to do this research before you travel to give yourself a clearer idea of what you want to buy when you are there. Your research will give you a sense of what a good value is, what a good price is, what any local scams are, and which details to look for. Our trip to Turkey would certainly involve buying a kilim (thin Turkish carpet) and our research helped us to understand how to determine good quality, the best cities to buy them in, and how to deal with shipping—the latter two areas were things we had not considered. We accomplished our research in a number of ways—first, we pinned an image from a page that described what to look for in handmade carpets and how to tell machine-made from handmade. This is another example of a pin acting as a bookmark leading to more information. We also looked at the prices available buying online and having the item sent to the USA—this gave us a basic price to beat if we wanted to purchase while in Turkey. When you have an idea of what you want, you can pin the applicable images to your board.

Learn About Local Cuisine

Part of the joy of travel for us is the food. Pinning dishes to your board will help remind you to seek them out when you are there and familiarize you with the food names. We found it useful to do two-fold research here before pinning images. First, we read very generally around the topic, isolating the things we really wanted to try. Second, we looked for reviews of good places to eat that served these dishes. We ultimately ended up pinning from restaurant homepages and sites like Yelp and TripAdvisor, but we had done most of the research on general topic pages (like Wikipedia and personal blogs).

Research Accommodations

If lodgings and accommodations are not pre-arranged, Pinterest boards can be great for gathering a shortlist (and ultimately final list) of places you plan to stay. You might like to pin lots of ideas from your research and then pare the list down. When pinning, we found it useful to include some description notes of what we liked about the place (the reviews and ratings, the images, the price, the location etc.). These notes can be especially helpful in making decisions directly from your board and not having to navigate to numerous web sites again to compare these details.

Share Local Information

Making a board about a place you know well might serve many purposes. There are countless boards on Pinterest about places people want to visit and maybe your home town could be one of those places. People have used place-based Pinterest boards for things like helping visiting friends plan what they want to do before they arrive, promoting a place that's special to them, or just for plain old nostalgia. Our board on Dave's home town of Hastings in the UK, is an example of such a nostalgia board. It was a lot of fun to assemble this board and think of all the things Dave misses about the place and all the things he thinks everyone should know!

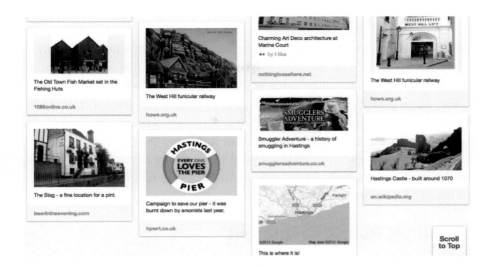

Charming Art Deco architecture at Marine Court
◆◆ by I like
nothingtoseehere.net

The Old Town Fish Market set in the Fishing Huts
1086online.co.uk

The West Hill funicular railway
hows.org.uk

The West Hill funicular railway
hows.org.uk

SMUGGLERS ADVENTURE
Smuggler Adventure - a history of smuggling in Hastings
smugglersadventure.co.uk

Hastings Castle - built around 1070
en.wikipedia.org

The Stag - a fine location for a pint.
beerintheevening.com

HASTINGS LOVES THE PIER
EVERY ONE
Campaign to save our pier - it was burnt down by arsonists last year.
hpwrt.co.uk

This is where it is!

Scroll to Top

Guidebooks will tell you the must-sees for any place in the world, but Pinterest boards can really leverage the hard-to-get local knowledge and hidden gems that guidebooks just miss. Guidebooks also become dated very quickly and will often miss the hot new things in town, whereas a Pinterest board can be updated in 30 seconds. These boards can also serve as nice resources for day-trippers who want a quick snapshot of the place rather than an in-depth description. With these kinds of boards, it is a good idea to pin from the Internet directly— remember, if someone is interested in your pin, being able to click through will allow them to get deeper into the content that interests them. However, you should also be aware that if you are following someone else's board, then you will be relying on them to update their content regularly.

This kind of board also offers you the opportunity to support local businesses. Shops and hotels, and even many museums, are often owned by local small-business people who don't have large advertising budgets. Word-of-mouth local recommendations are something they rely on, and Pinterest offers you the opportunity to support these local businesses.

Include a Map

A map is good thing to place on the board as it tells the follower exactly where this place is. The follower might find himself nearby and might not know your place exists. Free services such as Google Maps and Mapquest won't allow you to pin a map image to your board, but you can take a screenshot of the map and upload that from your computer. It's nice to search these sites for a map that provides followers the right amount of context—maybe you want to show your town or city in relation to a more well-known one, or with geographical markers (like county names, rivers, or lakes) also visible.

Highlight Points of Interest

The must-see sights and those that only the locals know of are excellent things to pin. As much as possible, it's nice to pin these from official sites because then your follower or repinner can click through to get details like opening times, ticket prices, and more detailed location information. For privately owned attractions, especially the lesser-known ones, linking directly to their site will increase traffic to their web site, which helps them improve their search engine ranking and visibility on the Web. Sometimes you'll find that official sites have poor quality images that don't make for very nice pins. In these cases, it's nice to make sure the non-official site offers readers a link to the official page; sites like Wikipedia are very good at doing this.

Include Places to Eat

Eating is something everyone loves to do and something where your local knowledge will be much appreciated. Most of the time there are lots of different ways to pin places to eat. If the venue has a web site, you can pin something from there. This has the advantage of allowing your followers to click through and see first-hand details on hours and location, as well as being able to get the latest menus and prices. If the venue holds any awards or official ratings, try and pin from the awarding organization (see our pin on the Jali Indian restaurant pinned directly from theaa.com). This pinning allows followers to learn quickly that venue is highly rated. Another nice idea is to pin via an independent site that aggregates and ranks restaurants (like tripadvisor.com). This kind of pin allows followers to click through and see independent reviews. If tripadvisor.com does not have an image to pin, but you live near the venue, you can take your own photo, upload it to the review web site, and then pin it. You could even take a photo of your favorite meal in the restaurant and pin that.

Jali - Best Indian food in Hastings

theaa.com

The Wild Mushroom in Westfield

webbesrestaurants.co.uk

Pin Local Events

Local events are usually only advertised well in the community that is hosting the event rather than nationally or even internationally. This makes them unlikely to lure in visitors from very far afield. It's a shame that these local events aren't advertised more as they often capture something unique to a town or city's culture. Typically, local events revolve around a niche interest—festivals related to local produce such as garlic and artichokes are two examples from where we live. For someone with an interest in the theme or agenda of the event, a pin could provide the inspiration to visit a particular place. This is where we feel Pinterest really sets itself apart from other social networks—with other networks you may learn about an event if a friend decides to post about it, but Pinterest is primarily set up to encourage *you* to search for what *you* are interested in. This approach makes local event discovery more likely! If fact, if you are involved in the organization of a local event (maybe through your PTA, a religious organization, or sports team for example), why not set up a board specifically for that? You'll find more details on that in Chapter 11, in the section "Promote a Local Event."

Highlight Local Hikes

Local hikes and walks make excellent pins. What's so great about them is that you can tempt people with a fantastic view and maybe a few key details, and then let them click through if they like it. It might also be interesting to include any guided tours that are available.

Add Links to Photo Archives

Pins don't always have to be in the here and now—photo archives are instantly engaging and make a great addition to your local page. Historic and vintage photos can be appealing to many different types of followers depending on the motivation behind their interest in your board. A follower might be a person with a connection to the place, but who has never visited. A follower may equally be a person who remembers the place from childhood and wants to be reminded of that. On our board, we chose to pin an archive of the town's Golden Era, a time when large portions of Victorian England flocked from the smoggy cities to enjoy a day of healthy sea air. A good source for images like this is historypin.com.

Include Tidbits of Popular Culture

Sometimes a city or town's claim to fame might be a key contributor to bringing in visitors—residents of Forks, Washington (the setting of Stephenie Meyer's *Twilight* books) will know this well enough. If this is the case, you would certainly reference this on your board—although you would also want to highlight the other attractions available to visitors.

   In most cases your city or town may not be referenced that much in popular culture, which might make this aspect of your board less prominent. As with our town board, we thought of these pins as hidden gems; a little serendipitous note that followers may not have expected.

Most places have had a famous resident at some point, or something of note may have occurred there. Why not pin something about this? On our board, we noted a popular TV series—*Foyle's War*—that was filmed in Hastings, and also documented some buildings that had notable residents at some point—fortunately various societies in the UK place plaques outside such buildings, and these make great pins!

Highlight Local Causes

In our opinion, most boards of this nature focus on what the creator thinks others should know about the place he or she is documenting— what they should see, where they should eat, where they should stay, and so forth. And in the spirit of promoting your town or city and supporting local businesses, why not also promote a local cause? Local causes and charities can generate significant online support and momentum through social media, and it seems fitting to mention these on your board. Maybe there's a charity that does great work in your area, or a building of local importance that needs restoration. On our board, we promote the campaign to save the local pier (which was burnt down by arsonists). Support from campaigners via social media has been key in pushing the local authorities to address the issue.

Using Your Own Photographs and Videos to Make a Gallery or Travel Journal

There are lots of sites out there that allow you to upload your personal photos and organize them into albums, so why would you use Pinterest to do this? Ultimately, there are benefits and drawbacks to choosing Pinterest as the place for your personal photos. We will outline both sides of the argument as we see it for both, but ultimately the choice is yours to make.

Understand Competitors and Make Your Choice

When deciding where to place your photos there are lots of things to consider. Of course, you don't have to limit yourself to one service, but in all likelihood you don't want to go through the process of sorting, captioning, and uploading your photos more than once. So you may want to think about which service you are going to use in advance.

There are some very good image-hosting web sites on the market. Two of the most popular are Flickr (from Yahoo!) and Picasa Web Albums (from Google). Both are free to use and both have excellent amounts of storage—although Picasa Web Albums offers users unlimited storage of photos under 2048 × 2048 pixels and videos under 15 minutes, and 1GB extra storage for larger items for free as opposed to Flickr's limits of 300MB and two videos per month. Both will also sell you upgrades for more storage space. But conceptually these are very different from Pinterest—image-hosting sites are designed as a storage facility with lots of integrated features, including sharing and editing functionalities. Pinterest on the other hand is purely designed to be a sharing vehicle. The point we make on this is not to assume Pinterest will keep and store your content for you. That said, although Flickr and Picasa Web Albums can help you recover data that you lose or delete, you should always *always* back up your data and store it on a flash drive, external hard-drive, CD-ROM or all of these. Assuming that you are wisely creating backups of your image files, we see no reason why Pinterest won't function perfectly well as your online photo gallery.

The other site to consider is Facebook, which has an image batch upload, basic editing facility, and no stated maximum capacity. Facebook makes it easy for your friends to discover your images with limited effort needed on your part. One point to consider with Facebook (and also image-hosting web sites) is that they retain certain rights over your content. You can configure your privacy settings to limit these rights, but it's complicated and couched in hard-to-read legal definitions and statements. Pinterest, however, is designed for sharing and unlimited discovery. So you should not be placing things on a board if you do not want them to be seen by people outside of your social network. Facebook also makes it hard for you to retrieve your data, should you wish to do so. You can request a compressed (ZIP) file of all of your Facebook data from the web site, but it can take a while to get the email directing you to the archive.

Understand the Benefits of Using Pinterest for Photos

If none of the previous paragraphs put you off and you decide to go with Pinterest for your photo albums, then here are some of the additional benefits. Your photos will reach a wider audience with no effort on your part. Through likes and repins you will get built-in feedback on your photos from other users. This may not sound like a benefit, but the Pinterest community is generally much more appreciative than communities on other sites (YouTube, for example). To date, we have not seen any negative comments on any pins, indeed Pinterest etiquette forbids this. Therefore, any feedback you get will be positive and offer you encouragement. The other benefit to using Pinterest is that you will be making a contribution to the community— Pinterest's growth and future depends on contributions for its community, so it's very rewarding to do your part.

Another benefit to using Pinterest for your personal photos is the notion of having as many things as possible all in one place. There's a clear trend in the tech world of users moving gradually to a more app-based Internet presence—that is, each individual having a preferred application for each need in their life (like Yelp for local information, Fandango for movie information, and so on). Given that social media touches all aspects of our lives, the large social companies continue to acquire products that cover gaps in their own services— Flickr and Picasa were both acquired to improve Yahoo! and Google's offerings in online photo storage and Facebook's recent purchase of Instagram appears to be targeted the same way. What is clear from a user perspective is that having accounts with 20 different services for essentially similar things is a pain. So having Pinterest as your photo gallery site eliminates the need to maintain (at least) one additional account (see Figure 6-2).

Maximize the Capabilities of Pinterest for Photo Galleries

We found it useful to change the file names of images to include a date and description, such as 7sept_GoldenGate. This allows you to

Click here to add a description

33 photos | 3 views | **Add a comment?**

items are from between 20 Aug 2010 & 21 Aug 2010.

Cake at the Madonna Inn

By David Todd (Albums) · Updated over a year ago · Taken at Madonna Inn, SLO · ✎ Edit Album

Figure 6-2   *Flickr, Facebook, and Pinterest photo boards*

understand quickly what the images contain when you are browsing to choose your upload. If you have not already done so, you might want to create a folder containing only the images you want to upload, rather than having to sort through a folder of hundreds that you aren't going to upload. Here are a few more tips:

- *Work backwards.* Currently, Pinterest displays your pins in the same order you upload them—and you cannot move pins around on a board. So the last thing you pin will be the first pin

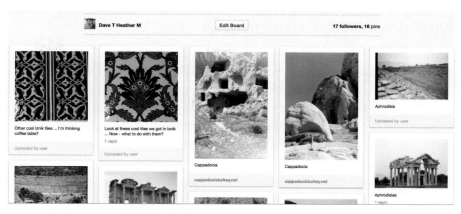

Figure 6-2 *Flickr, Facebook, and Pinterest photo boards (continued)*

shown. This means that if you wish to order your travel gallery in a particular way, you will need to have planned it out before you upload. As primitive as it sounds, we used a pen and paper to accomplish this. We used the file-naming convention mentioned in the previous paragraph to determine the order of the photos and crossed each one out as it was uploaded. This is painstaking work, but the impact on your board will be huge.

- *Offer outgoing links.* One of the great features of Pinterest is the ability to add a link to a photo you upload. It's really good for travel journals because you can show people your photos and offer them a link to more information about what's in the photo. We found travel guide web pages, Wikipedia, and official web sites great for this purpose. It's great for someone viewing the photo and wondering what the building and place is to be able to click through and have their questions answered.

- *Pin other stuff.* You can get a really interesting travel board going by not limiting it to just your photos and videos. You might like to take photos of things you bought and add those to your board. If you have a scanner, you can scan things like tickets, receipts, a brochure to an attraction, or a postcard. All of these things will add a little flavor and identity to your board, making it more like a scrapbook!

Make an Announcement

If you have a big announcement to make, definitely use Pinterest
for it! Some examples of announcements we've seen on Pinterest are
engagements, weddings, new babies, and graduations. The great thing
about announcement boards is that, if done creatively, they have instant
impact and can look so much nicer than ordinary photo galleries—in
fact many end up looking like photo collages you would hang on your
wall.

   The previous section focused on using personal photos in a more
general sense, but here we will look at using editing software and
utilizing the Pinterest grid structure to make a board that is designed
to be seen as one piece of work, rather than as a collection of
individual pins.

Understand the Pinterest Board Structure

The way Pinterest boards are templated and their basic formatting is
important to understand in advance of creating an announcement
board. Each board is set up in a grid pattern by default which you can
take advantage of to display images. The number of columns your
board will have depends entirely on the size of your browser window,
your monitor size, and your screen resolution—most people see
between three and five columns. Almost every image you upload or pin
will have some sizing information—you can see this information by
right-clicking the image and clicking View Image Info. The relative
sizing of your images will affect how they are shown on the board—big
images will be kept big and so on. If you have images of exactly the
same size, they display as neat rows and columns, as shown in the
following illustration of our birth announcement board, rather than
the collage look of most Pinterest boards.

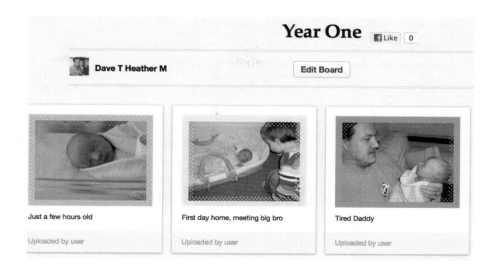

Year One Like 0

Dave T Heather M   Edit Board

Just a few hours old

Uploaded by user

First day home, meeting big bro

Uploaded by user

Tired Daddy

Uploaded by user

Get Your Images Sized Correctly

In general, it's a good idea to resize images you take with your digital camera before you upload them to the Web. Most cameras are capable of taking very high-resolution images, which isn't necessary for Web use and will take much longer for you to upload. Most probably your camera came equipped with some basic photo editing software, but if not, free image-editing programs can be downloaded from sites like cnet.com. If you want the images to display in a neat grid pattern on your board, do the following with your image editor:

1. Open your image editing program.

2. Select Resize or Resample from the Edit menu. Your editor may have this function in a different menu but most basic programs have a resize or resample option.

3. Select image dimensions to resize your image to. You want something around 400 × 600 pixels or possibly less. If you aren't offered an option to choose from in your editor, enter a number in the first box (i.e., 300 pixels); the height or width should adjust automatically.

4. Select Save Image As and name the new file.

5. Repeat the process for any subsequent photos taking care to make the exact same adjustment to each.

If you are going for the fixed grid approach, you might like to select photos that are the same layout (either all portrait or all landscape) for the effect to work best. If you are keen to have one special photo that doesn't fit in with the others included in the board, you can use your image editor to change the layout to one that will work.

Add Some Flair to Your Images

One way to get some real spark into your board is to add some additional decoration. You might want to try adding some colorful frames around each photo. By default, whatever picture you upload or pin is surrounded by a white square or rectangular frame. If you add a frame before you upload the image, you add a splash or color to your board and make it more than a simple image gallery. It will actually look more like a personalized photo greeting card and give the board so much more character.

Again, your digital camera probably came with a basic image-editing program that gives you the option to use frame templates. If not, you can easily download free software from the Internet.

Consider Using Other Types of Images, Not Just Photos

You may want to pin your own photos into your announcement board and that can look great. However, you can give your board a little lift and variety by adding illustrative images as well—wedding bells for wedding announcements, storks and rattles for a new baby board, and scrolls and graduation hats for graduations all work well. Try to find images that suit the look and feel of your board —in our experience, cheap clip-art never does a good job.

In order to add these types of illustrative pins you will need to save the images to your computer first. This is so that you can resize them if you are taking a grid approach. Also, if you want them to have a particular type of border, then you will need to do that in your editing program.

Add Text but Keep the Pins Uniform

You will naturally want to add some text to accompany each image of your board. If you want to keep the images the same size, make sure you enter the same amount of text beneath each image when you pin it. If one image has two lines of text and the rest only have one, the image with longer text will display differently.

Get the Order Right

As mentioned in the "Maximize the Capabilities of Pinterest for Photo Galleries" section, the first pin you upload will be the last one displayed in your board. So upload pins in reverse order. For example, if you have twelve images that you want to display in chronological order (say, baby photos from one day old to 12 months old) upload number twelve first.

7

Building Boards for the Home and Garden

Boards for the home and garden are very popular on Pinterest—you can find all sorts of inspiring ideas from simple projects to do with kids to large-scale DIY projects that only the most adventurous among us might dare to undertake. This chapter looks at different board ideas from leisure activities like crafting, to design-oriented projects like planning and documenting your home improvement ideas and revamping your garden, and even managing a few of those mundane, day-to-day tasks like organizing your recipes and making shopping lists. You will see how using Pinterest boards can not only organize and streamline your planning of major projects, but also make you more efficient in your everyday life.

Plan Craft Projects

According to the Pinterest analytics site Repinly, DIY and crafts represent the second-most popular pins (behind food and drink). What this tells us is that Pinterest is a great resource for finding all kinds of crafting ideas. This is hardly surprising if you look at some demographic details available on Pinterest users—50 percent have children and 68 percent are female—a key segment of the crafting community. It's also not surprising if you look at what people like to pin and repin—crafting is always represented in the high repin counts.

Help Buzz travel "to infinity and beyond" with this rocket ship-shaped "star globe."

family.go.com

Stencils for fabric. Nice idea for pillows and place mats

cuttingedgestencils.com

Hedgehog craft made out of microfiber car washing mitts.

dollarstorecrafts.com

Photo star craft

homemade.tipjunkie.com

This section focuses on sharing ideas for gathering and organizing great crafting content that appeals to you. It also focuses on thinking beyond just pinning craft ideas.

Use Pinterest as You Craft

Making crafts is something we typically do in different stages rather than all in one go. We've often had the inclination to do something crafty with the kids, but by the time we find something engaging, head out to the craft store for things we invariably don't have at home, and print everything out, then the moment has usually passed. Pinterest can make this process easier.

If you think of a Pinterest board as a visual bookmark for something you might want to do later and pin to it whenever you come across a nice idea, then the research is all ready when it comes to craft time. The pin will also serve as a visual reminder of the things you need to buy for the craft, so you can build those into your daily errands. The result is that you will be managing your craft prep more effectively (when *you* have time) and can then jump right into doing the crafts when the moment takes you. You'll also likely be able to save money by replenishing your craft supplies at your convenience (and when things are on sale), rather than purchasing specific items in a hurry for immediate use.

Find Good Resources

The good news for the crafter in you is that Pinterest is loaded with cool craft ideas. It is easy to search directly with Pinterest, using the pin or board filters to find content with that personal recommendation you are looking for.

 You can also find things with a little more "wow" factor using Repinly, which identifies popular pins by the number of repins.

But, if you don't find anything that really grabs you on Pinterest, you can always try searching the Internet. When searching the Internet for craft ideas, you can avoid a lot of the junk on a search engine results page by searching within known good quality sites (like marthastewart .com and kaboose.com). If you are searching for crafts related to particular brands, movies, TV shows, or characters, official homepages (like disney.com) have such pages hidden in their domains—using the internal search or site map can help you to drill down to these pages. If you are searching for something more specific or a little more unusual, you may have to rely on a web search, but using the image search options can guide you a little quicker through the mass of results.

Organize Crafts by Purpose or Event

While many people seem to have one general craft board they pin to, this might not be the most effective way for you to use Pinterest in your crafting. If your aim is to be more organized and more effective in your planning and execution of craft projects, then why not segment your projects and ideas into multiple boards? This will allow you to develop and view more focused project areas rather than having to look at everything craft-related at one time. You could segment your crafting boards by purpose, setting up boards for crafts for home, crafts for school, and crafts for a birthday party. You might also like to set up boards for crafts by occasion, like Halloween, Valentine's Day, or Thanksgiving. Unfortunately, a fantastic craft idea you see for Halloween in March is lost by the time October arrives. Using Pinterest lets you save this idea for a later date.

Pin Techniques and Other General Reference Material

Other useful things to pin to your board are craft techniques and tips that not only apply to a particular project, but also are good general resources to keep track of. We always seem to struggle with getting papier-mâché right, so we pinned a good resource for this onto our board. Additional things you might like to pin are guides to certain types of products, describing which one to use and for what purpose (like pencils, scissors, and paints).

Document Your Crafts and Add Improvements

While most pin board content will come from the Internet, you could consider uploading your own photos of craft projects you have undertaken. Sadly, in our house many of the crafts we make with the kids deteriorate or get thrown out at some stage—really, keeping craft projects around indefinitely is hard as the fun is mostly in making them. So, taking a photo and uploading it to your board is a nice way to document and preserve the craft without cluttering up your living space. You can then share the project with friends and family members who follow you on Pinterest.

Consider using the comments field more extensively on your craft pins. You can invite feedback from those who see the images on Pinterest. More experienced crafters may be able to guide you in your technique and friends and family might write some words of encouragement for you! You can also use the comments field to clarify instructions on a craft project, indicate how you customized a project, or document any issues you faced while making the craft and things you might do differently next time.

Get Ideas for Supplies

Use your craft boards to collect ideas for craft supplies—the things you will need for specific projects and the things you need to have on hand all the time. You might like to visit your favorite stores' web sites and pin directly from there. You may also find ideas for recycled craft supplies and things you can gather from your garden or a beach. Either way, this board can be a place you check before you go shopping for supplies, or after you choose a craft to make. Think of it as an inventory of what you have mixed with a shopping list of what you need.

Plan and Document Home Improvement

Home improvement is another very popular category on Pinterest and you will find lots of boards crammed full of inspiration. When creating a board for home improvement you may want to take one of two approaches—keep it general or make it specific. This will allow your board or boards to perform their different functions instead of being cluttered. By its very nature, a specific board—where you create an entire board based on one project—would ideally be dedicated entirely to that one project so it is easy to read and follow. More general boards would likely contain lots of small projects that could each be conveyed in one pin, or a range of ideas and projects you are thinking about doing. For example, we recently used a Pinterest board solely to plan how we wanted to hang pictures on the living room wall—having the one board dedicated to this was very helpful as it was a complete project in our minds. We had the pictures and the wall; we just needed to organize the arrangement. When looking at a bigger topic, like an entire room remodel, we found it more helpful to start with a general board of design ideas, which we then refined down to what we could actually do.

Make a General Ideas and Inspiration Board

Inspiration boards (or boards of things you simply really like) are one of the most popular on the Pinterest site—and the home décor category is full of such boards. Find fun and interesting things you like and pin them to a categorized board. In this case, people dedicate a board to the home and pin everything they like there. You can create this kind of board quite freely, as it's not aimed at any specific project—in fact it might even contain things that are entirely impractical for your living space. The board is really an expression of what you like and find interesting. Some popular things to pin to this kind of board include furniture items, design patterns, techniques, and tips—whatever takes your fancy!

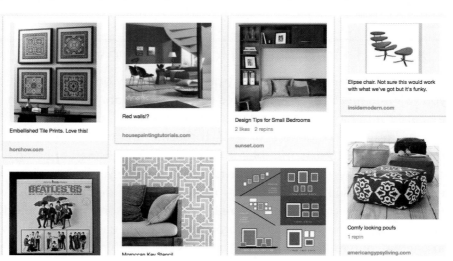

You'll find many commercial stores are developing a Pinterest presence. This obviously makes great sense for them as they can get their products in front of people with a declared interest in the topic—something online marketers can rarely do with such accuracy and in an unobtrusive way. Right now, Lowe's Home Improvement has a great inspirational Pinterest presence with ideas on all kinds of home improvement projects and style tips. Rather than scouring the Web, you may want to just poke around on their page and repin things you like from there. Of course, there's no commitment to buy from Lowe's, but if you want to, you are nicely linked through your pin.

Make a Specific Project Board

While a general inspiration board helps you develop the overall flavor of a design project, a specific project board gets you into the nitty-gritty details. Your board can function as a practical resource for your project that is easy to locate and not hidden among your other pins. A project may be large or small, but having everything on that one board is definitely very helpful when it comes to actually doing the project itself. It might also be the case that an inspiration pin turns into the starter pin for a particular project, so don't be surprised if a project board grows from a somewhat random pin.

A large project that you make a board around might be something like remodeling or redesigning a room. For these projects you could start thinking in a wider sense to begin with—looking at the space, pinning the elements you want to get into that space, and trying to set a tone for a specific look and feel. Once you have those pieces in place, you could move onto the large furnishings, flooring, and wall. Finally, you could close out with the finishing touches like decorations and accents.

In terms of resources on large space-based projects, you might start with some kind of space planner program—Ikea has a great free tool online that you can use to make a basic measured plan of the space. However, you will have to take a screenshot of your plan and pin that to get it onto your board.

One thing that is great to pin onto a project board is a technique or tutorial. The Web is full of great sites that can walk you through each stage of a tricky task. As you plan a project, you will probably be aware of things you know are going to be a challenge for you as you are doing them for the first time—the techniques and tricks videos will be a very useful resource for you when it comes to doing the work.

 A wonderful site for finding techniques and how to's is www .thisoldhouse.com.

Another aspect of preparing for a project is making sure you are equipped with the correct hardware. There are lots of places you can pin products from—your favorite hardware stores likely have a web site, and many online vendors also deal in tools. You might also want to check out some review sites for more objective opinions on the products.

Document Your Work

Posting pictures of your home improvement work is a great way to enjoy and share what you have accomplished. A fun idea is to show the before, the inspiration, the during, and the after. This way you can really see the whole project end to end. Make sure to have your camera on hand at all times to allow you to document things frequently—if you have a smartphone that supports a Pinterest app, this is perfect. In the example shown in Figure 7-1, we had a wall and some pictures, but no idea how best to hang them. We followed the suggested layouts, moved the cutouts around, agreed on a configuration, and hung the pictures. The whole process took a few days, most of which was spent moving the cutouts around and seeing how they looked. We were very pleased with the results!

Covering a dull wall with our Middle Eastern treasure ... Before -> During -> After

Uploaded by user

Figure 7-1 *Home project at various stages*

Plan Gardening Projects

Gardening and yard projects are an evergreen topic on Pinterest—pun intended. This means you will always be able to find great ideas and plenty of motivation to take on the yard from looking around Pinterest boards.

More so than other kinds of projects, gardening requires meticulous planning. Virtually everything we want to do with planting requires research into the correct time of year, optimal spots in your garden for each plant, and which plants will thrive in close proximity. If you are planning on building or renovating in your yard, then you'll need to look into the best techniques, materials, and tools needed for this work.

Much like home improvement, you can either create one large gardening board, or break each project into its own dedicated board. We like one board per project because it focuses your efforts and keeps things that are not relevant to that project out of sight. However, one board showing what you started with and what you have achieved is a really great idea too.

Create a Board for Inspiration

Using Pinterest to make an inspiration board is a great way to get yourself motivated and to help you decide what you really like. You'll find a wide variety of garden ideas and styles on Pinterest and if you keep pinning the images that appeal to you, you may soon find that the garden of your dreams will reveal itself on your inspiration board. You don't need to be particularly restrained because these pins are only ideas and thoughts, not things you will definitely do. Later, you can do a small reality check to make sure you are not heading in a direction that has no chance of being realized—if you live somewhere with a cool climate, then a garden full of bougainvillea isn't really ever going to work.

Outdoor/garden tub? Yes!!!!!
19 repins

goodlongwhile.typepad.com

Plants to attract bees and other pollinators
11 likes   58 repins

sunset.com

more green canopy ideas
2 repins

invitationtotuscany.com

Look Out for Themes Developing on Your Board

As you create an inspiration board for your gardening project, you'll probably start to notice themes developing—maybe your board is telling you that you are particularly interested in vegetables, maybe flowers, maybe a garden in a particular style (like Japanese Zen or English Cottage). You may find that you're more drawn to lively, colorful gardens than tidy, serene gardens, or succulents and cacti rather than roses and boxwood. When you reach this point, it's a good sign that you can stop casting the ideas net too wide and begin to focus your efforts around your chosen elements. You may want to keep the inspiration board as it is for future reference, or you may prefer to delete those things that aren't relevant right now in order to turn the board from an inspiration board into a planning board.

Things to Think About as You Plan Your Board

Once you understand the general direction of your board, you can start to apply this to the garden that you have. As you will discover, your geographical location, personal tastes, views on conservation, and general experience and handiness will have a huge impact on the way you go about developing your board and garden. To help you on your way, here are a few things to consider.

Research Your Area

As much as anything, the area you live in—particularly its USDA zone, climate, and water availability—will dictate what kinds of plants you can or cannot have. You may also wish to create a garden that is easily sustainable and directly conscious of the natural conditions in your area. As residents of California, we wanted to have a garden that did not require heavy watering despite high summer temperatures. This meant we had to research drought-resistant plants like cacti and lavender that can survive in arid places. We also have very busy lives, so low-maintenance plants make a huge amount of sense to us. Of course, your own local geography may be very different, so if you live in a cold or rainy climate, you will want to make sure what you are planning can accommodate that. You may have a good chunk of time to dedicate to maintenance, so you can plan for that too. If you have plans for a themed garden, you could focus on which plants work well in your area and fit the theme.

As you become aware of your environment, you can use the comment field of your pins to incorporate aspects of a gardening calendar onto your board. You will need to figure out good seasonal planting for where you live and you can add these kinds of notes to your board. Try to think about good annual versus perennial plants that will thrive where you live. You can also consider when the best time to plant different vegetables and fruits is and track your success with each crop.

You may also want to consider whether you want to develop separate seasonal garden boards that outline what you will do as the weather changes. Maybe you want to have one board for the summer, one for the fall, and so on. A summer garden will be very different for vegetables and fruit gardeners in particular.

Make Use of How-to Videos

There's a lot of really useful advice online, so if you are planning on minor or major landscaping projects, you may wish to make use of it. Even simple tasks, like making a raised bed, require thought and planning. By pinning how-to videos to your Pinterest gardening boards, you can benefit from others' successes and know-how.

For more advanced projects—like building a patio, deck or walkway—these how-to videos will be essential. Even if you are pretty handy with home improvement tasks, these videos will arm you with other essential information, such as the best types of materials to use, good positioning, and useful tools to invest in.

You can also leverage how-to videos for garden maintenance. One consideration for our garden was learning how to compost organically—the tutorials were very helpful. We also learned a lot about how to fight bugs and weeds organically. There are countless gardening sites that offer videos including organicgardening.com and garden.com and you can also find videos on YouTube or by searching Pinterest.

Refine the Look and Feel of Furniture You Want

There's a wealth of garden accessories and furniture on the market, so you'll have plenty to sort through. Once you have your theme well-developed, you'll be able to narrow down your searching for the right furnishings and accessories. If you are putting together a Mediterranean garden, then you might like to look into wrought iron. If you are going after an Asian look, then maybe bamboo is right. You can also then start to think about wall hangings, statues, fountains, and many other finishing touches for your garden. If your garden is about renovation and renewal, you may even want to explore the idea of refurbishing any existing patio furniture you may have.

Document and Share Your Success

As always, it's great to share! Think about taking before, during, and after photos and pinning them sequentially to show everyone what you have achieved. Maybe also include the pin that inspired you and gave you ideas. Pinterest is all about sharing, and maybe you will inspire someone else to make their pins a reality.

Organize Your Recipes

Although many of us have a collection of old recipe books on a shelf somewhere, nowadays most of us use online resources for the majority of our recipe research. Good online recipe sources offer everything that cookbooks offer and more—including user reviews, video instructions, and the ability to filter our searches by many different variables (time to prep, time to cook, complexity, and ingredients, to name but a few). The challenge becomes keeping track of all the recipes you discover online.

Several years ago we started a scrapbook of recipe clippings we had printed or cut out and had liked. We simply filed the recipes into a clear plastic binder and kept it with the cookbooks. This presented us with a number of problems. First, the binder had no index page as it was being constantly added to—this made it difficult to remember what was in the folder (and where it was). Second, the recipe papers we usually placed on a counter top when cooking often got stained. Finally, any comments we noted were largely unreadable when we came to review them as they had been scribbled in haste as part of cleaning up the kitchen. What we needed was a place where recipes could be added in a structured way, where neat and tidy comments could be added, and where none of them would get damaged or lost. And then along came Pinterest …

Pinterest is absolutely perfect as the online recipe cataloging device because it overcomes every drawback of managing your recipes offline. In addition to solving all of the issues we mentioned with the recipe scrapbook above, it offers some other advantages. For starters, it's highly visual (in fact, it is almost impossible to pin a recipe without an image). Also, the limited character count forces you to be clear in your notes and keywords. It is also worth remembering that because Pinterest is social, it encourages you to use recipes that your friends and people you follow pin. Finally, Pinterest allows you to make use of video content on recipes sites. If you own a laptop computer, tablet device, or even a cell phone, you can take that video right into the kitchen with you.

Build Different Boards for Different Types of Meals

One of the greatest benefits to having Pinterest be your recipe archive solution is that you can control the indexing in a way that suits you. By

Figure 7-2 *A board of family-friendly meals*

categorizing recipes into types that make sense to you, you can effectively build that recipe book that was never published—"things *my* picky kids will actually eat" is one example that jumps to mind, or family meals that are easy to pull together (see Figure 7-2).

You might want to think about organizing your boards in the same way a recipe book does. One advantage Pinterest has over cookbooks is that it lets you add and delete whatever you like, making your recipe reference sections more personalized than any book could ever be. Different ways to organize your recipe boards might be by:

- **Cuisine**   For example, Italian recipes, Chinese recipes, Thai recipes.

- **Main ingredient**   For example, fish, tofu, chocolate.

- **Course**   For example, desserts, starters, finger food.

- **Diet type**   For example, low-fat recipes, South Beach Diet recipes, vegan recipes, gluten-free recipes.

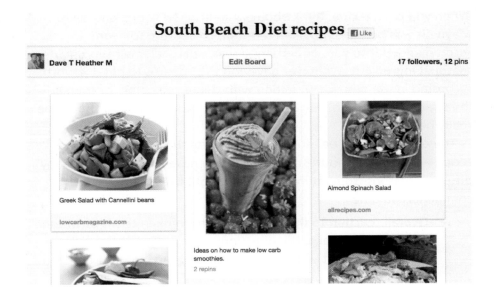

- **Occasion**   For example, holiday recipes, picnic recipes, kids' party recipes.

Create a Dream Recipe Board

The ever-popular "someday" board can also apply to food. You may like to build yourself a board full of things that look fantastic but that you think you might never actually attempt—or at least may attempt at a much later date. Having this type of board is also great because it'll encourage you to keep these ideas away from your everyday functional recipes, making your "to use" boards much more functional and free of clutter. You can always come back to these later on when you are feeling more adventurous.

Use the Descriptions and Comments to Maximum Effect

Given that you are building these boards for your own use, you can really maximize the text fields to make your board even more helpful.

When you pin a recipe, think about what inspired you to choose it. Maybe it was because you liked the chef, or because someone recommended it to you, or perhaps it was a particular occasion or seasonal ingredient. Whatever gave you the impetus to pin it is worth recording in the description (along with the recipe name, of course)—in fact, the description may help you to decide which board the recipe really belongs on.

The comments can be especially useful after you've tried out the recipe—we often annotate recipes after we have used them for many different reasons. Some things that you might like to add to the comments could be

- **Overall reaction to the recipes**   Try to think in terms of whether it was easy to make, the directions were poor, if it lived up to expectations, if it yielded the number of servings indicated, and so on.

- **Ingredient substitutions**   It's pretty common to make substitutions based on what you have on hand in your pantry. The comments section is a tidy place to note these for your (and others') later reference.

- **Ingredient locations**   If you have a recipe that requires an unusual ingredient, you might like to record where you found it. This could be very useful if you want to make it again.

- **Other feedback**   If you are open to other people's feedback on your cooking and meals (and you may quite reasonably not be), you could encourage those who tried the dish to add to the comments section too. Even if they haven't joined Pinterest, they can comment on a pin. It'll provide a nice way to reference what people do and don't like.

Capture Recipes from Magazines and Newspapers

If you are someone who discovers new recipes from print sources rather than on the Internet, don't be discouraged—there are lots of ways to get that content onto your Pinterest boards. Perhaps the best way is to

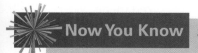

Now You Know **Search Within a Web Site**

Sometimes a web site's search functionality is poor and difficult to use. Many times, we have used a web site's search box only to be sent to a regular search results page rather than a page of results from that web site only. If you find it tough, you can simply search with a search engine and restrict the results to a given domain. To do this, type *site:domain.com* at the end or beginning of the query, leaving a space between the query and site. For example, *butternut squash site:sunset.com* will give you all the results for butternut squash from within the sunset.com domain only.

check whether that publication has a web site. If it does, you may be able to find the recipe there. If that fails, then you could scan the recipe and then upload it. You need to think about this very carefully though as you will need to include directions and ingredients. You could either include them in the image, checking that they are readable when you scan, or type them out in the comments section. Typing them out is time-consuming but offers better legibility.

Include Related Boards

In addition to boards of recipes, you may want to create boards that are useful references for your recipes. These might include things like videos of cooking techniques or tips or even a wish-list of kitchen equipment that you need to make your recipes.

Use Pinterest to Plan Family Meals

There are many reasons for planning family meals—in our household it makes grocery shopping more effective, eliminating last-minute dashes to the store, avoiding the need to get take-out meals, getting a balance into everyone's diet, and reducing the stress of figuring out what you are going to cook when meal times come around. Like many ongoing household tasks, the more time you put into planning, the more efficiently you'll be able to manage the task.

There really is no shortcut to planning regular, organized meals. We have tried a simple paper list on the refrigerator, meal-planning software, and a calendar dedicated entirely to meal times. Each of these methods works in its own way, but each also has a flaw that has caused it to fail for us. We ended up really liking Pinterest for meal planning because it overcame each obstacle. For example, the software required you to have your computer around you at all times—even in the store, which is not practical. With the Pinterest mobile app on our phones, on the other hand, the meal plans are always with us. We tried dedicated apps for meal-planning (like Meal Planning by Food on the Table), but it became yet another application we had to keep checking in with and was entirely detached from anything else we did. As we were using Pinterest for so many other things, it made sense to use it for meal planning as well. The paper lists and calendars were OK too, but they got dirty, buried under the numerous school notices and coupons on the refrigerator, and on one occasion lost outright. Losing the plan after the effort put into it was soul-destroying. The lists were also not very inspiring and we had a tendency to deviate from the plan because of this. Fortunately, these factors, which thwarted our planning attempts, were all resolved by using a Pinterest board (see Figure 7-3)—it never gets lost or dirty and is always inspiring and the recipes behind the pins will be linked, making it very easy for you to work quickly.

Figure 7-3   *A week's worth of meal plans*

Follow These Tips for Meal Planning on Pinterest

As we said earlier, you need to dedicate quality time to the task of meal planning to make it most effective. Make sure to carve out an hour or so when you will not be disturbed, distracted, or too tired to give it the attention it needs. Here are some other tips to keep in mind:

- **Set a realistic goal**   If you are able to plan out a month's meals in one session, then you are a better person than either of us … and probably better than anyone we know. For most of us, a week at a time is realistic. Defining what you are attempting to achieve will focus your efforts and provide satisfaction when it's complete.

- **Work on a clear surface**   Try creating a new board solely for each week of meals. That way you can see everything at one time, without even having to scroll around.

  If you do this week after week, you will end up with dozens of boards that will be hard to find on your Pinterest boards page— Meals for Week of 7/30, Meals for Week of 8/6, etc. For this reason, when you are ready for a new week of planning you might like to do a review of the previous weeks' meals and repin some of them to the upcoming weeks. We'll talk a little more about how to reuse and recycle pins later.

- **Pin in reverse**   This is mostly a cosmetic thing dictated by Pinterest's current functionality—specifically, displaying pins in the order in which they were added. We like our pins to display Monday through Sunday for this kind of board, therefore we have to pin Sunday's meal first, Saturday's second, and so on. If you can live without this organizational trick, then great.

- **Write specific comments and titles**   When choosing a name for each meal, try to use fewer words and make the words you use reflective of the purpose of each pin. If this is a weekly meal planning board, then each pin will likely be a meal for each day, so the text should capture this. In our weekly meal boards, we start with the day of the week it is for and the name of the dish (for example, Friday—Meat loaf). The great thing about this is that you just scan the board quickly and click where you need to.

- **Try to use keywords in your titles and descriptions** Using good keywords, ones that you will remember, will make it easier for you to find things using the Pinterest search functionality. Making clear and concise descriptions and titles will also help other Pinterest users to discover your pins.

  We also like to draw attention to the things we will need to buy for these recipes. It's possible to include the whole ingredients list, but that text will lose its structure and become a jumble. It's also pretty pointless to clutter the comments box with certain ingredients that we always have around (milk, salt, baking powder, etc.). Because of this we like to add a comment to each pin saying "Need to buy:" and listing the things that we don't typically have on hand.

- **Make use of previous work** If you have already taken time to pin recipes you like to a recipe board, then by all means reuse these in your planning—this is work already done after all! Try looking at your existing recipe boards as part of your planning process. If you see something that would work for a meal for next week, repin it then and there.

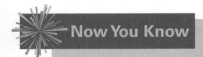 **Now You Know**   **Save Time on Typing Your Descriptions**

You can save a lot of time getting ingredient lists into the comments field by highlighting the list on the web site before you pin. Highlighting the text will automatically add it to the pin description box before you submit the pin. However, we don't always want the text in the description—we want it in the comments field. So we can cut the text (using CTRL-X) from the description field before we submit the pin, type out the actual description we want (day and meal name), and click Submit. We can then view the pin, click the Comment button, and paste the text (using CTRL-V) into the comments field. You can then submit the comment.

- **Note successes**   Be sure to make comments on things that were successful. Maybe a certain meal works well on evenings when dinner needs to be earlier, later, and very fast. You can then rotate these in as your schedule determines.

Build a Shopping List with Pinterest

Before we get too far into this usage of Pinterest boards, we need to make it clear that this really only works for certain types of shopping lists. Your weekly grocery shopping is not one of those uses. The thing with grocery shopping (for the most part) is that what you really need to buy doesn't require a pin to explain it—peanut butter is peanut butter. You should also consider the effort making a board would take each week when just writing or typing something could suffice. The final drawback of the grocery list is that you can't organize the pins within the board, so you'd be scrolling around forever as you walked through the grocery aisles.

This brings us to the fantastic uses for Pinterest boards for other kinds of shopping lists. The most wonderful way to use Pinterest for a shopping list is when you are not sure exactly what you want but have a rough idea. This usage works well when you intend to research online and buy offline, but also works for researching offline and buying online. It's worth noting that you really need to have the Pinterest app installed to your mobile device. Check out Chapter 5 on mobile pinning to learn more on this.

Research Online and Buy Offline

A common situation for us is that, while we are happy to buy online, sometimes we really want to see the item in person before handing over the cash. For example, if you are buying a piece of furniture you might want to check if it lives up to the expectations—images online can be deceptive. You might also want to measure the item yourself, rather than trust the listing measurements. Another situation might be that you need the item now, and don't want to wait however long it will take to be delivered (and the hassle of having to be home all day waiting for the delivery). An additional benefit is that you may get a better deal in-person—once shipping costs are removed and print coupons applied. But the final reason, in our household, is the most common—you can't really find exactly what you want online and hope you will know it when you see it in-person. In all of these cases using a Pinterest board can help you leverage that online research in your local stores.

If you are planning to use your board because you want to see the product in the flesh, then go ahead and pin it to your board from the store's web site—this will allow you to click through on it if you need to and show the most current online price and shipping times and costs. Some stores will give you the online price in the store if it's lower so you can sometimes save money by having this information at your fingertips. You might also want to write down the questions and concerns you have on the product too, so you remember to resolve these in the store.

Aviator glasses

shop.nordstrom.com

Diesel shorts

raffaello-network.com

Canvas slip-ons

shop.nordstrom.com

A Grey Stripe

abercrombie.com

If you are in the position of knowing roughly (but not exactly) what you want, then you can take a much wider approach. You could pin as many examples of the product or type of product you are looking for. It could be very helpful to use the comments and descriptions fields to make notes on what you like about it, how it is not quite what you want, how much this example is, and where this example can be bought—these will be useful comparison references while you are shopping. A great example of how this board can work really well is when using a Polyvore board as shown in Figure 7-4. This site allows you to create an outfit online and pin it to your board. You have the option to buy the outfit

Like {0}

Tweet

<> Embed

Report Pin

@ Email

summer cool, created by davetandheatherm on Polyvore

Add a comment...

Figure 7-4   *An outfit with accessories created on Polyvore*

through the vendors selling on Polyvore, but there are many reasons you might not want to do this—price could be one, another could be that not everything in the outfit is exactly right for you.

If this is the case, why not take the pin to the shops with you and see if you can do better? Using your mobile Pinterest app, you will be able to re-create the outfit in your favorite stores and take it home that day. You can reference the pin while shopping to get similar items to those Polyvore recommends, but also to compare your prices.

Research Offline and Buy Online

As the title of this section indicates, this is really the reverse of what was described in the previous section. This usage of the Pinterest shopping board is helpful if you see something while you are out shopping, but aren't convinced enough to buy it. Perhaps you think you can get a better price elsewhere, you want to keep looking, or because you have no intention of buying it right now. In each of these cases, using your mobile app to pin an image of the product helps you create a shopping board that you can use for further research from home or even while you're still in the mall!

A scenario we are all very familiar with is shopping for an outfit for a special occasion. You walk around most of the mall looking at things and trying them on, take a lunch break and try to remember everything you saw, go back to the stores and buy more things than you need, then come back a few days later and return most of what you bought. It's exhausting and time-consuming. Using a Pinterest board, you can pin each thing you try on—if you are shopping with someone, you can even have them snap a picture of you with the item on (if you are alone, then take a picture of yourself using the changing room mirror). You can make a note of where the item was and how much it cost using the comments and description fields. By the time you get to your lunch break, you'll have a whole board of everything you looked at ready to review. If you can make your choices based on that board, then you are all set. However, you will also have that board to take home and review—maybe you want a second opinion, maybe you want to see if you can find better deals online, or maybe you just make clearer judgments after taking a break from the shopping. Either way, you will have a board ready to help you make your decisions.

8

Building Boards for Career and Study

U sing Pinterest boards for career and study may not be the most obvious application to many people, but it really can work. While there are pluses and minuses to using it over other applications, Pinterest offers the flexibility of using many different types of content. We have also found it really helpful to get as many of your tasks and projects into one place as possible, so we don't have to keep switching between applications. For example, having your latest résumé on Pinterest makes it easier to find, rather than having it in a documents folder.

In this chapter we explore how you might integrate Pinterest into your professional life. We look at ways educators can organize their teaching ideas on a Pinterest board, take a simple reading list and turn it into a rich resource hub, or visualize a school curriculum by moving it over to a pin board. We also explore using Pinterest to build a career by defining the job you want, documenting your past accomplishments, and creating a visual complement to the standard paper résumé.

Use a Pinterest Board to Organize Teaching Ideas

If you're a teacher you probably tend to think a lot about your students in your free time and likely have dozens of favorite web sites for different subject areas, teaching strategies, or cool project ideas to try with students.

It's fairly common when you have lots of links to bookmark them in your browser, but it makes them very difficult to find because with many browsers (Internet Explorer and Firefox especially) all you have is a small amount of text to recognize them by—and if you don't carefully name the bookmarks when you create them, it becomes very difficult to know what anything is. Even with browsers that have visual bookmarking (Safari, Chrome, and Opera), your bookmark is a small snapshot of the whole page and it can often be difficult to recognize what that page contains.

Pinterest is an ideal way to organize all that teaching inspiration in one place because it will give you visual results and fuller text descriptions to remind you of what lies beneath each pin. Pinterest does lack the folder structure of browser bookmarking and the ability to move your bookmarks around on the board, but we have found that the larger image-based format of Pinterest and the larger text fields make it a lot easier to navigate and read.

It's also worth noting that using Pinterest boards for organizing classroom ideas can be applied even if you are not a professional teacher. Parents, tutors, and school volunteers can also benefit from researching some techniques and ideas to make sure you are giving good guidance.

As with many topics, you may want to start with a more general board for a broad range of teaching ideas. If you have a particular need for a more specific topic, you can break that out onto another board.

Creating a General Ideas and Activities Board for Teaching

If you are just starting to get your teaching ideas onto a Pinterest board, then a general board is a good place to start. You can start by thinking of favorite or recommended activities for the subjects you are teaching. You might like to find ideas and activities that are versatile enough to be recycled for different teaching points or that focus on general teaching techniques and classroom management. The general board is also a good place to pin all those articles you want to read, but haven't gotten around to yet.

Create an Ideas Board for a Challenging Content Area

If your students are having difficulty with a specific area of the curricula, you could pin ideas from trusted web sites that you think might help your students. If you are struggling to find ideas for sources you know, you can try searching Pinterest for ideas from other people, or even try searching the Internet in general. Another valuable resource for you will be your friends and colleagues who are teachers. For example, a teacher friend had students struggling to understand the difference between Present Simple and Present Continuous in English. We found some of our old worksheets with practice exercises that our friend was able to scan and pin to her board.

When you talk to your colleagues, friends, or other parents, try pinning their ideas and strategies to a board as a way to brainstorm. Our example board of teaching kindergarten reading skills was put together using advice from teachers, things that have worked for us in different teaching settings, and ideas shared by other Pinterest users.

Consider Sharing Ideas with Colleagues and Pin Their Ideas

If you are in close contact with other teachers, either those in your classroom or other teachers on Pinterest, you might like to try connecting with them through Pinterest and sharing ideas there. If you know of a teacher who has taught a group of students before or faced problems teaching a particular topic, you can ask them for ideas. If other teachers allow you to contribute to their teaching board, you could also try sending things that have worked for you directly to another teacher's board (see Chapter 4 "Create a Group Board" for instructions on how to do this). This is a great way to generate new ideas for your students and to let other educators know what's worked and what hasn't worked in your classroom at the same time.

Share Suggestions and Ideas with Parents

If you are in contact with parents regarding their child's education, you could try helping them out via Pinterest. Parents often ask teachers where their child needs a little extra help and how to help them at home. In these situations you could easily share some of your pins with the parents to help them work on certain topics from home. If they are registered on Pinterest you can ask them to follow you and you can mention them in a pin that is relevant to them. If they are not registered, you can send them a link to a pin. It's worth remembering that parents who are involved in what their children are learning can help reinforce any emerging skills like reading and arithmetic—sharing ideas with them can help to encourage this.

Consider Whether to Involve Your Students

This is a tricky area because you don't want to blur the lines between school and social lives. Remember also that your Pinterest account is publicly accessible and tied to your email or Facebook account. Also, you should find out if your school has a policy on social media and contact channels that prohibit the kinds of interaction we outline here. Weigh whether or not sharing boards with students is a good idea at all given your teaching context.

If you are permitted to go ahead with involving your students on your Pinterest boards, then it could be a powerful tool for you. Sometimes this kind of personal attention from a teacher can be appropriate and hugely beneficial and provide some real motivation to your students. Keep in mind that everything you post on Pinterest could be viewed by all of your students. For example, if you have a board on classroom management for sixth-graders, you won't necessarily want your students to be privy to some of your more subtle techniques.

 You must avoid including any pictures of your students on the boards for obvious reasons.

In terms of reassuring yourself, it's worth remembering that Pinterest policy explicitly says that nothing inappropriate or illegal can be posted on boards—this makes it less likely that students will encounter wildly inappropriate content on the site. However, some of the content is of dubious value and may not be something that parents want their children exposed to.

Try Breaking Out Your Boards into More Specific Topics

Once you have assembled a general teaching ideas board, the next logical step is to break the board out into smaller, more focused areas. This will allow you to find the content you want quickly, rather than having to sort through hundreds of pins. Some great ideas for the more specific boards are

- **Specific topics in the curriculum**   You might like to make a board that focuses on some smaller part of the whole curriculum. For example, you could break out a math board into a separate calculus board.

- **Classroom management**   Try dedicating a board to the craft of teaching and dealing with common situations. You might also like to dedicate a board to managing inclusion effectively and supporting learners with special needs.

Figure 8-1 *Autumn- and Halloween-themed ideas for the classroom*

- **Projects for seasons, holidays, and celebrations** You could try looking at your curriculum and cross-referencing when certain topics will be taught with seasonal/cultural events like autumn and Halloween, as shown in Figure 8-1.

- **Classroom decoration** You can make use of the countless numbers of decorating boards to get inspired for new and engaging ways to decorate your classroom.

Make a Reading List

The idea of using Pinterest for making a reading list is a very handy one for many different groups of people, regardless of age and educational setting. In this section, we explore how moving a reading list to a Pinterest board can help you to process what you need to achieve, dig up useful sources for getting the books, supplement your reading list with other types of information (like quotes and study guides), and use the comments field to share help and advice with others on the same course or program. We will also look at non-academic uses for reading lists on Pinterest for those who read for pleasure.

Make Reading Lists for Educational Uses

As a student, putting your academic reading list onto a Pinterest board will, in a short space of time, turn a dull written list into an appealing, visual, resource-rich hub that will benefit you throughout your studies. Getting a reading list onto a Pinterest board can help you process and understand the list a little. From our experience, part of what makes a reading list overwhelming is that it is a page of book titles that takes a minute to read but translates into a great many hours of actual reading. By turning the list into a Pinterest board, you go through the process of doing a little initial research into the reading material that will help you understand it better.

Be Creative in Finding Good Sources for Your Books

Two great things about books today (and a huge difference from when we were at school) is that they don't exist only in print form and there are many easy ways to get them. With this in mind, you should consider looking at the different sources available as you organize your board—in many cases you can pin directly from the source itself and save yourself time and money. We have found the following techniques very useful:

- **Pin from your library web site**   Using libraries is, of course, a no-brainer because they are, thankfully, free. If you have access to a school library, then it is probably the best place to start as it stocks multiple copies of books on recommended reading lists.

However, most cities and counties in the U.S. have public libraries with online catalogs so you can make use of these as well. Many allow you to place a hold, check availability, and receive notices when the book is ready for collection. This will help you with scheduling and planning too. Library details such as ISBNs, library call/index numbers, editions, and general availability are good things to add to the description field of each pin.

- **Look for free online books**   If you are on a budget it's good to utilize as many free resources as possible, such as organizations that catalog books that are out of copyright, like Project Guttenberg. Using these resources requires you to be comfortable reading from a computer screen, so if you are not keen on this then you could avoid these sources. Unfortunately, sites like Project Guttenberg don't contain images, so you have to be a little creative in how you pin these. We recommend using Pinstamatic, a site that allows you to pin a snapshot of a web page and link to that page. See Chapter 5 for more details on this.

- **Utilize any e-reading device you have**   E-readers like the Amazon Kindle, the Apple iPad, and the Barnes & Noble Nook are readily available and now considerably cheaper than when they were first introduced. One of the great things about these devices is that they often offer electronic books at a cheaper price than the printed editions. In fact, if you are looking for classic titles, they are often free because they are out of copyright. If you are planning to use an e-reader, then you can pin your book titles directly from the sellers' e-reader bookstore.

- **Shop around for things you can't get for free**   If you have exhausted all other resources, then you can start looking for the best deals to buy the books. Try to do a little shopping around, and then pin from the site that offers the best price.

Supplement the Books with More Useful Information

Once you have gathered and sourced your books, you can begin to add useful information. Things you might like to add are

- **Other books that help you understand the one you have to read**   This might include critiques of the work, study notes (like Cliffs Notes), and articles about the book.

- **Quotes**   As you are reading the books you may like to pull out some poignant quotes for future reference. You can pin these using Pinstamatic.

- **Web sites**   Again using Pinstamatic, you can pin useful web sites and reviews of the book to your board.

- **Author information**   It can be useful to add background information on the author.

Use the Comments Boxes to Engage with Other Students

If you have classmates who are following a similar reading list, you might like to encourage them to make comments on the books on your board. You could get some nice exchanges here that help everyone to understand the important themes and events in the books. You could also ask them to add additional resources to your board that will help the whole group.

Make Reading Lists for Recreational Uses

Even if you are not following an academic program, you can still make a reading list board. There might be many different themes or purposes to your board, but that's for you to decide. Some popular boards that we have seen are vacation reading, books to read, and favorite books.

Vacation reading lists are great because pinners typically pin popular, up-to-date, light books. Given that many people like to pick up a couple of novels at the airport for their vacation reading, using a Pinterest board to get ideas and see what others have liked might help you make good choices in the bookstore.

Listing books you've read is usually something that one does on a personal blog. Using Pinterest, however, means you can do this without having to set up and maintain a blog. When you are making a blog entry, adding links and images is somewhat time-consuming, but Pinterest makes this so much easier with a few clicks and relatively no typing.

You might also like to use Pinterest simply to list your favorite books. You could do this in a very unrestrictive way, pinning books that you love from all categories—from childhood favorites like Dr. Seuss to modern novels. However, it might also be fun to dedicate boards to your favorite books divided by genres. You could, for example, list your favorite children's books—this could prove to be an awesome resource for you if and when you have children of your own, nieces and nephews, or grandkids to read to.

Plan a Curriculum

When we were teaching, individual curricula were, at best, handed out as sheets of paper at the beginning of the year. At worst, we were given a textbook that had no curriculum, just a table of contents. In either case, a curriculum is determined and communicated to the teacher, but it's up to the teacher to translate that into teaching points. Whatever your teaching situation, you will find that transferring the curriculum onto a Pinterest board can help you to plan the year, term, or semester ahead quickly and easily, by consolidating your existing resources and finding new ones.

As we've said before, sometimes the simple act of creating a Pinterest board will actually help you to digest the task you are trying to perform a little quicker, without taking up a huge chunk of your time. Because Pinterest boards are created by pinning directly from the Web or uploading your own images from your computer, putting your board together requires you to do some research to find what you want to pin. This in turn forces you think about what is a high-quality, appropriate source for each thing you are pinning, and so helps you to dive into the body of the topic in some finer detail. If you have worksheets on your computer or popular links already bookmarked, you can start by pinning from these resources right away.

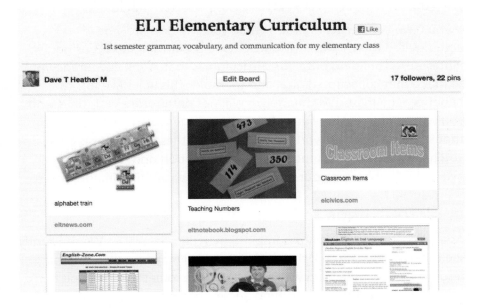

Try Working Backwards

Because Pinterest will always place your most recent pin in the first position on the board, you will need to work backwards on your curriculum if you want it to run chronologically. In our example board of an English Language Teaching curriculum for elementary learners, we had to cover five modules in one semester. So, we started at the bottom of the semester's curriculum (Module 5) and pinned module by module in reverse order—this means that material and ideas related to Module 1 appear at the top of the board. Using this approach feels a little counterintuitive, but the result is a board that runs from the beginning to the end of the semester, which gives you a really strong sense of how the semester needs to progress.

Once you have started organizing by modules or sections, it might be useful for you to consider pinning materials that complement each other consecutively, so that they appear next to each other on the board.

Incorporate Your Own Accumulated Ideas

If you have been teaching for a while you will definitely have accumulated lots of paper resources. One great thing about using Pinterest for building out your curriculum is that it will encourage you to make that collection digital and sharable. This will have lots of benefits—the materials themselves will not deteriorate with time, and you will be able to share your teaching experience and legacy with thousands of teachers worldwide. Digitizing these resources is easy if you have access to a scanner, which many schools and homes have available. Simply scan your papers and pin the resulting image files.

Look for Things to Repurpose

As a teacher, you probably see inspiration in unusual places. We constantly see things on the Internet that we think would make excellent teaching resources on non-teaching web sites. If you see something that you think you can repurpose with a teaching angle, then go ahead and pin it. For example, when planning the curriculum for a class for ten-year-old elementary English learners we came across a page of Johnny Depp characters, all with wacky hair and make-up. Students of this age know and love the kinds of movies that were featured in the article and so we added this piece to the board with a note to use it for describing physical appearance.

Top 10 Best Johnny Depp Characters -
Great for physical description
language

1 like   6 repins

tiptoptens.com

Look for Seasonality

As you plan out your curriculum, try to think about when you will be teaching each item. You can then consider what will be happening at that time in your students' worlds and look for tie-ins. For example, our elementary learners will be working on describing body parts right around the end of October, when all the Halloween decorations will be going up. We added a great activity for describing monsters to do at this time.

Share with the Teaching Community

As always, the greatest benefit to having your curriculum and ideas on Pinterest is that you can share with fellow professionals worldwide. You might want to consider opening up your board to other pinners that you know, so that your colleagues can add ideas that they find too. You will also be well placed to send a pin to another teacher who is looking for inspiration on a certain topic.

Find a (New) Career

A Pinterest board can be a great visual aid and resource in a career or job search. You can not only pin your résumé, but also use the board to showcase many other things about you.

If you are looking for a social web site where your résumé will be viewed by recruiters in your industry, where work experience, qualifications, and references are what you want to showcase, then that site is LinkedIn (linkedin.com; more on that later). Right now, the majority of recruiters are not searching Pinterest for résumés, but there are still many career-related things you can do on a Pinterest board.

Start with General Ideas

Pinterest boards can be very useful if you find yourself at a career crossroads. Sometimes we find ourselves not really knowing what kind of career we want. Try thinking about things that interest you professionally (or even just in everyday life) and start pinning away. You could start by thinking of companies you like or admire or places you would love to work. Check these companies out online by looking at their official sites. Sometimes you'll need to look for the corporate web site to read about the company from an employee perspective—you can often find links to these corporate sites at the bottom of the retail/commercial homepage. If you like what you read, then pin it! Pinning a corporate logo or brand will be instantly recognizable on your board. You might also want to think about what inspired you to pin this company to your web site—is it something they sell, the way their image appears to you, something you like about their ethos? You can type this information into the pin description. In no time at all, you will have a visual record of what kinds of businesses you like and why. Maybe you can then focus your career aspirations and start looking for opportunities in those industries.

Aside from company web sites, you may also want to think about products, services, or even people that interest you professionally. Following the approach mentioned above might also help you understand what you are interested in.

Add Your Résumé

Adding your résumé to a board dedicated to your career is a good first step; however, it's unlikely to be the most engaging pin on your board. There are a few ways you can do this. If you have a web site where you can host your résumé, pin from this. Make sure to include an image in your résumé, navigate to the web site, and pin the image. The image will then link to your web site's résumé page. If, like us, you don't have a web site, then you can upload your résumé from a file on your computer, as shown in the pin in Figure 8-2. Pinterest does not support text documents like Microsoft Word or Open Office Writer, so you will have to convert it to an image file. Here's how:

Figure 8-2 *A résumé uploaded as a pin*

1. Open your résumé document in Microsoft Word.

2. Take a screenshot of it by pressing the Print Screen (PRTSCN) key at the same time (COMMAND-SHIFT-4 on a Mac).

3. Open Microsoft Paint and press CTRL-V (COMMAND-V on a Mac) to paste the screenshot.

4. Use the Crop tool to highlight the actual document area (the screenshot process will capture everything seen on your computer screen, not just the document).

5. Press CTRL-X (COMMAND-X on a Mac). The highlighted area will disappear.

6. Open a new Paint document and paste the document in by pressing CTRL-V (COMMAND-V on a Mac).

7. Save the file as a JPEG.

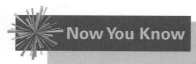

Now You Know **Create Screenshots for Things Larger Than Your Screen**

If your résumé is more than half a page, you will not be able to get all of it in one screenshot. If you reduce the document size, the resulting image will not be readable. To overcome this you can take multiple screenshots and use the Cut and Paste functions in Paint to merge and align each portion.

Pin Examples of Things You've Done

If you are lucky enough to have an image or Internet link to things you have accomplished or produced in your career to date, then you can add these to your board too as shown in Figure 8-3. Sometimes it may be hard to find things to pin, but here are a few things we've seen on other boards and some things we've pinned to our own résumé boards.

As writers, we've been able to pin some of our blog posts, as well as links to books we've written. If you have written anything, or even been quoted or credited in an online article, you could pin that to your board.

For those of you that design or make things for a living (or even a hobby), why not pin examples of those to your board? We have a friend who makes purses and jewelry boxes and sells them

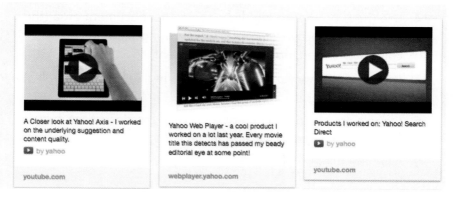

Figure 8-3 *Pins of projects you've worked on*

online—these make excellent pins for a career board. A professional photographer we know adds example of his photographic work to his career web site. Whatever it is that you do for a living—if you can photograph or video it, then you can pin it!

You may also want to document companies you've worked for. It's worth making sure you use the description field to describe the pin, as readers may be confused as to whether you actually worked at this place or would like to work there.

Integrate Conventional Career-Based Social Media

If your intention is to get noticed on Pinterest by prospective employers, and even just to generate contacts or leads, then you may want to consider integrating a profile from somewhere like LinkedIn. What could be worse than a potential employer finding your work on Pinterest and then not being able to contact you at all? I chose to integrate my LinkedIn profile because this contains all of my recent work experience and my recommendations; a prospective employer would easily be able to learn a little more about me and contact me using this profile.

In order to pin a profile, you need to have an image or video to pin. In my case, I used my photo from my profile. I then added the profile link in the pin description in case someone didn't realize they could click through.

 Anyone can see a Pinterest board or pin, so make sure there is nothing in your pin that you would not want in the public domain (like street addresses, phone number, or email addresses).

Part III
Discover Collaborative Project Ideas

9

Make Boards for Communities

In previous chapters we've mentioned getting other people you know involved in your boards. In this chapter we focus on the type of board you can make to include a *community* of people, who will actively engage with the board and bring their own content to the community.

The communities boards we talk about in this chapter, such as club boards and genealogy groups, require members to join Pinterest in order to pin to the board; this is really no different than an online forum or web community. But Pinterest provides benefits over other types of community sites—most notably the ease of pinning articles, images, and videos and the higher prominence given to these media over text.

Another added benefit of having your community home pages on Pinterest is that you will have a greater opportunity to be exposed to other similar communities. As Pinterest is a sharing community itself, your pins and activities will be shown to many other pinners—which could lead to more followers, perhaps new members, and maybe even the possibility of mutually beneficial contact with similar groups in other areas.

The final upside we have found is that once you connect with similar communities and start to follow their members and their pins, you automatically will be exposed to content relevant to your community via the "Pinner you follow" section of your Pinterest page.

Create an Enthusiasts' Meeting Place

Let's start this out by defining what an enthusiasts' meeting place might be. We would define enthusiasts as people with a declared interest in a specialized area. Typically, collectors are a good example of this—they might be collectors of porcelain, sporting memorabilia, or stamps. More typically, though, they have a specific interest within a narrower category. For example, we have a friend in the UK who collects soccer pins, but only those containing an emblem of two crossed hammers (which appear on his favorite team's badge). We have a family member who collects foreign coins, but is particularly proud of his collection of obsolete European (pre-Euro) currency. In a similar vein, porcelain collectors may be interested in pieces from a particular period (for example, art deco or art nouveau), a particular manufacturer (Wedgwood or Royal Doulton), or even a combination of the two.

Badges with Hammers   👍 Like

This board is dedicated to football pin badges that contain crossed hammers. This is inspired by my team, West Ham who have had the crossed hammers on their crest since 1895. Does your club have these? If so, follow me and I'll make you a pinner so you can add yours.

Dave T Heather M   [Unfollow]   18 followers, 0 pins

Shakhtar Dontesk - Ukraine

Zonguldak Spor - Turkey

boleynbadges.webs.com

Glanshammars IF - Sweden

boleynbadges.webs.com

boleynbadges.webs.com

Aside from collectors, enthusiasts can be people with very specific tastes in a given field, but the things they are interested in might not be collectable per se. You might find movie enthusiasts with an interest in a specific genre or director. There are also people with interests in architecture or design. "Foodies" are some of the most dedicated enthusiasts as they devote themselves to enjoying and sharing great food and drink.

Beyond the scope of most individuals' boards, community boards that serve as a meeting place for a group of enthusiasts can attract a more dedicated group of followers who will more actively engage with each other and share their own content, extending both the reach and depth of the board.

 If your interest is as a business owner seeking to reach out to your clients, then you may find lots of helpful tips in this chapter on building and developing a community through Pinterest. However, the responsibilities of hosting a community board for your business are much greater than those of hosting an informal community. You might need to consider tasks like running a marketing campaign, launching a promotion, and keeping your inventory updated. Information on boards used for business purposes can be found in Chapter 12.

Define Your Topic Clearly and Build Up Your Community

We encourage you to approach this type of board differently from those mentioned previously in the book. Your intent here is to target the board to a particular community. This community might (and in the early stages will) be very restricted—but you can change that as your board takes shape. With this in mind, you should tailor your board to suit the niche interests of those you want to attract as followers and pinners. A good place to start this is in the description box. Clearly state in this box exactly who this page is intended to benefit, and what your expectations are in terms of who should pin and what they should pin. This will help to draw the kinds of people you want in your community.

With a specific description and pins that are clearly labeled and of good quality, your online following should start growing immediately. You might also like to consider using a hashtag when you set up your board and add your pins. This will make your content more easily discoverable to like-minded enthusiasts as they will be able to use it to help them find things that might be appropriate to your board. You can also use it to search against in the event that other pinners start using it. See "Use Hashtags in a Pin" in Chapter 4 to learn more about this process.

If you think people you already know may be interested in the board you are working on, you could try grabbing their attention on other social media sites, such as Twitter and Facebook. The easiest way to do this is by linking Pinterest to these social media accounts. For a reminder on how to do this, see "Control What You Share on Facebook and Twitter" in Chapter 3. Depending on how keen your friends are to contribute actively to a board, you could consider allowing them to add pins directly. Instructions on creating boards with multiple contributors can be found in "Create a Group Board" in Chapter 4.

Pin Images of Interest

Your enthusiast's Pinterest board should contain specific, focused content on a level that reflects *your interest and knowledge*. This will attract followers who are at the same level of interest as you, so you should not feel that you are expected to research and include details beyond your comfort level and time-commitment.

With this in mind, start pinning what you have to show and share! Depending on the topic, this might entail a fair amount of prep work. If you collect something physical (like porcelain, sports memorabilia, or stamps), then you will need to digitize your inventory. For some collections you may simply be able to photograph the items you have and upload those photos to your board. Remember to photograph things that other collectors might be interested in—for example, with porcelain the manufacturer's stamp is of just as much importance as the item itself. For other collections, such as maps or baseball cards, you could consider using a scanner to digitize your items. A scanner allows you to get higher-quality images than using a camera. Additionally, some scanners use a feeder, allowing you to scan many items without having to place each one individually. You could also consider using the Pinterest mobile app to do everything quickly from your mobile device—you may need to do some photo editing in a different app, but it is an "all-in-one-device" solution, so there is no need for cameras and memory cards.

 The effort to digitize your inventory is well worth it. Digital copies can be very useful if you ever want to sell anything, if anything is lost or stolen, or if you want to take stock of your collection without removing things from their place of storage.

If you already have your items online, you might like to simply pin from your web site. Your pin will automatically link to your blog or web site and this holds the additional bonus of potentially getting more people to visit your site.

Pin Articles of Interest

In addition to pinning images, consider adding articles to the board. Articles can provide information relevant to your topic and add variety to the content of your board so it isn't all images. The following image shows an interesting example of a pinned article on a wine enthusiasts' board. A new vintage of a local wine was receiving rave reviews online, so the board owner pinned this article, using the article title as the description. The community members then used the comments field to discuss the article. Which leads us nicely into the next section.

Winemaker Notes 100% Estate grown fruit produced and bottled at Larkmead Vineyards 53% Merlot, 29% Cabernet Sauvignon, 10% Petit Verdot, 5% Malbec, & 3% Cabernet Franc Aged for 17 months in 55% new French oak barrels 902 cases produced

Luis J
Tasting Notes "Very deep ruby red color. Wonderful aromatic intensity - floral violets, black cherry, blackcurrant, sweet thyme & cedar then complex secondary notes of soy and game. Lively exuberant palate entry then immediate density of blackberry and cassis fruit. Bold, rich and youthfully assertive but retains inner-mouth perfume and energetic brightness. Lingering chewy tannins on a flavor-packed finish.

Utilize Comments for Reviews, Recommendations, Assistance

Given that you are using your board to interact with a wider community, you should really try to get the most out of the comments fields. There are many different things you can use these for, but we would encourage you to be proactive in soliciting comments from your community. A great way to do this is by asking a question, rather than simply describing the pin. For example, if you have a manufacturer's stamp on a plate that you can't identify, you could ask for help in the description or comments field—this will encourage those with that knowledge to communicate with you.

You can pin a product you recently tried out or share a brief movie or book review you've written. You can then ask others to share their opinions. Because of Pinterest's character limitations (maximum 500 characters), you'll find that people will post succinct reviews.

Pin Events and Deals

If your topic of interest has active communities outside of the Internet, your followers will likely appreciate pins about any relevant events (trade shows, festivals, etc.) or good purchasing deals (free shipping, seasonal discounts, and bulk-buy offers) that you come across.

Creating a Club Bulletin Board

At first thought, it might seem preferable to use a social site other than Pinterest as your club's home page or bulletin board. There are many ways that clubs exist online today—there are Facebook groups that allow you to control membership, post images and videos, and share articles and web pages of interest. There's also Meetup, an online social network that helps groups organize to meet offline. In our opinion, these sites work really well for groups where you want to avoid mass online visibility—that is, you want your group to have a restricted membership controlled by an admin and ensure that content you post is only visible to your membership. For some groups, a children's club, for example, this might make a lot of sense. However, for others this seems to be something of a limitation.

Pinterest works best for club bulletin boards in cases where you want to expose your club's activities and general existence to as many people as possible. As we've noted before, everything you pin on Pinterest will be visible to all users, not just those in your social circle. There are some limitations in the way Pinterest works that can make using the site for club bulletin boards frustrating, but we have found plenty of ways to work around these. The issues of free-form status updates and calendar events in particular are addressed later in this section. But once again, it's Pinterest's simplicity that can make this site work for all of your club's needs.

Starting Your Board

As with the enthusiasts' board, it's a good idea to use the board description field to state exactly who you are and what your board is for. Many people who repin or like your pins may never see this section. However, if people like your pins and decide to check out the board they are on, you want the description of your board to be clear to them.

Grow Your Club's Reach

Given that people are not currently using Pinterest with the same
frequency and in the same numbers as a site like Facebook, growing your
community online may take some time and effort and you'll need to be
prepared for it to build up slowly. Club members who are not already
Pinterest members will need to sign up for Pinterest and follow you
before you can add them as pinners to your board. Hopefully, you will be
able to evangelize enough about Pinterest to sell them on the idea.

To recruit followers to your club board, try using the comments fields
and repins to open up communication with other Pinterest users. An
easy way to do this is to make a comment on a pin before you repin it.
You should avoid being pushy or invasive, but you can compliment the
pin and say that you are repinning it to your club's board—for example,
"I love this knitting pattern—it's so original. I'm repinning this to my
knitting circle's board." The original pinner will be notified that they
have a comment and repin either when they sign in to Pinterest again
or via email updates (if they elect to receive these). There really isn't
any downside to doing this, only upside. From the original pinner's side,
they have a compliment, a repin, and a potential source for more

content they may be interested in. The original pinner can always delete or ignore the comment if they don't like it. From your side, you have gotten your group's name out there in the Pinterest community.

Point People to Other Places They Can Find You

Many clubs already have an online presence. You may have a web site or blog dedicated to the club. You might also use Yahoo! Groups, MySpace, or a Facebook group as a home page for your club. If you have an existing online location for your group, you might like to share these sites on your board, so that people can check you out there. All you need to do this is to pin an image from a page of the web site, blog, or Yahoo! Group that you are trying to link to. If you are looking

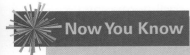

Now You Know | **How to Pin Your Group Page**

If you are unable to create a pin from your group page (or any page) directly, you can use this workaround to create the same effect. All pins are images or videos that ultimately credit their source, have a description, and link back to their place of origin—but all of these things are editable. You can take advantage of this by uploading a picture from your computer and editing the source and URL.

1. Find an image for your group that you would like to pin on your board.

2. Save the photo to your computer.

3. Upload the pin by clicking the +Add button at the top right of the Pinterest page, choosing Upload a Pin, and using the Browse button to locate your image.

4. Choose the board you want the pin to appear on by using the drop-down menu (by default this will show the last board you pinned to).

5. Write a description of the pin and click Pin It.

6. Once the pin is uploaded, find it on your board and click Edit.

7. In the box labeled Link, change the URL to your group's URL.

to make a pin from your Facebook group, you won't be able to do that because currently Facebook does not allow pins from their site. You could, however, use any image that represents your group and pin that instead (see the sidebar, "How to Pin Your Group Page").

Before you do any of this, make sure that the privacy settings on the site you're linking to will allow people to see details of what the group is and how they can join when they click the link. You don't want to frustrate an interested pinner by allowing them to click through to a page that doesn't give them the information they're seeking.

Help People Get Started in Your Activities

If your club is based on a particular skill or activity, it could be interesting for readers to see pins offering background information. In the case of a certain sport, this might be very generic information (like rules and history of the game), but if your group is engaged in activities with some interesting local context, then you could make pins that link to that kind of information.

Equipment recommendations and costs

Show local events   Provide background to your club

It can also be helpful to people looking at your board to get some idea of the costs involved in participating in your chosen activity. You might dedicate some pins to information about basic equipment and tools.

Pin Details of Upcoming Meets and Events

If your group meets regularly, you can make pins dedicated to upcoming events. Unfortunately, Pinterest does not offer any social calendar integration, so you will have to be creative about how you do this. One way to do this is simply by treating an event as you would any other pin—if your event is listed on a web page, then make a pin from there using any images available on that page. If there are no images, then find a suitable one from another source, save it to your computer, and upload it. You will need to make as many of the details about the event clear in the description, so your members and community will know what the pin is saying.

If you feel you want the date to stand out more than anything else, then you can easily achieve this effect using Pinstamatic. This site will allow you to make an iOS-style calendar pin for the date the event takes place. You can then add the appropriate URL and description to that pin. The beauty of this is that the pin will be instantly recognizable as a date, which would be synonymous with an event in most people's minds.

Save the date - Fencing in the park begins.

salledecesare.com

Send Pins to Particular Members

Much as Facebook allows you to share a posting to another person's wall or timeline, Pinterest allows you to recommend particular pins to other Pinterest users you are connected to. To do this, you simply enter the *@user name* into the comments box for that pin. For example, in order to recommend a humorous animal photo to Pinterest favorite George Takei, you would type *@George Takei* into the comments box for that pin. Once you start typing the user name, a drop-down menu will try to predict who you are looking for. Click the name of the person you want to recommend the pin to and submit the comment. This can be very handy for groups and communities when you want to send something to a particular person, but don't necessarily want to pin it to the group's board.

Pin Images and Videos from Recent Events

The most important thing to say about this type of pin is that it will probably be one of the staples of your board. Images and videos from events let readers know that this group is active, not solely an Internet community, and can give prospective members an idea of what to expect if they decide to join. If your community competes in any way (like my fencing club), these pins can inspire and encourage others as they represent goals they could try to achieve themselves! And for your existing members, these pins provide an easy way to maintain contact and interest.

When creating these pins, it's important to make the descriptions on the images and videos meaningful to both members and non-members. If you use too much jargon or too many inside jokes, you'll lose your wider audience quickly.

Remember, the more people that follow your board, the more you can share the workload with regard to uploading videos and photos by allowing others to pin.

HighlightYour Group's Appearance in Media

Occasions where your organization or members are mentioned in the media are another fun thing to pin to your club board. You might be lucky enough to generate some national coverage like one member of our fencing club who won a world championship medal, but any kind of coverage, from your local newspaper to a community newsletter might be worth pinning. Frequently, members of groups miss news articles and TV coverage, so pinning them to your board adds to the group's archives and gives everyone in the group a chance to enjoy each other's achievements and congratulate those in the limelight.

Make a Vacation Choice Board

In Chapter 6 we looked at making a vacation board for planning a trip we knew we wanted to take. We also looked at ways we could update the board post-vacation, turning it into a kind of online scrapbook. But, what if you have no idea where to go on vacation or what kind of vacation to take? In this section, we look at ways you can you use a Pinterest board to turn your vacation decision-making into a collaborative effort, encouraging you to set ideas out, ask for opinions from your travel partners, and gather consensus before reaching a conclusion.

The ideal starting point is having no idea where you want to go on vacation—from that position you can let your imagination run wild and pin everything you have been dreaming about.

Make the Board an Ongoing Project

Like many Pinterest boards, this type lends itself well towards continual development. Trying to narrow down the details of the exact vacation you plan to take will likely take you a long while because there are so many factors to include—time of year you can go, budget, and your desired duration, for starters. Choosing a vacation is often driven by your discovery of possibilities and ideas. From our experience, we typically get inspired by stories of other people's vacations—friends will post holiday photos on a social web site, or will tell you about their vacation at social gatherings. Other times we find inspiration in our general web browsing—typically a travel article somewhere on the Web will grab our attention and subtly cause us to think about that destination or holiday type. Sometimes we find inspiration in magazines, or just watching a travel show on TV.

The point here is that we frequently get ideas through our daily lives, and more often than not we make a mental note to think about it some more at a later date. Most times we never come back to these thoughts and the inspiration is lost. That's where Pinterest can come to your aid! Because of the ease of pinning things we find on the Web, we can document those ideas right away—it takes less than a minute to pin something while on the Internet. You might still have to get into the routine of adding pins based on conversations and ideas from other media, but again finding something to pin to capture that thought can be a very quick process.

By using this approach you will capture most of the fantastic ideas that cross your mind. As you build up the world of possibilities on your board, you can start to develop each pin and really enhance your board, before arriving at your choice.

Think About Different Destinations

The logical place to start your board is with the destination. You might like to think about countries if you are considering international travel, or more broad geographical areas (like the Pacific Northwest, for example) if you are looking to stay within the U.S. Sometimes, you might have a particular city in mind, other times a collection of cities. Whatever your thoughts are on possible destinations, it's very useful to pin them to your board. You might be able to combine a destination with other aspects of your vacation ideas later on.

Consider Ways to Travel

In addition to thinking about where you might like to go, thinking about how you might like to get there can add some variety to your board. There are all kinds of possibilities—flying, travelling by train, renting an RV, renting a boat, or taking a road trip, for example. You may see some connections emerge between means of travel and the destinations you've already listed. For example, if you have cited national parks as possible destinations, then maybe an RV vacation to a national park might work for you.

Pin Different Types of Vacations

Pinning types of vacations can help establish how much effort you want your vacation to be. If you find yourself gravitating heavily towards the all-inclusive beach vacations, perhaps you're really looking for a break where you can just unpack your bags and put your feet up. If you find yourself pinning ideas related to self-organized and self-directed vacations (like camping or road trips), then you may want to spend more time on detailed planning on sightseeing and activities. Understanding the level of physical investment you are prepared to put in can really help to focus your choices.

Explore Pricing of Vacations

Budget is likely to be a major factor limiting your vacation choices, so having this information on your board will definitely help to keep your choices realistic. The purpose of this board is to lay out options and make choices, so it doesn't really make sense to pin the all-inclusive Costa Rica trek if you are looking at a cheap family vacation for a week.

Price tags can be very easily added to your pins—you simply need to include the price (in the format $123) and the tag will be added to the top-left section of your pin. Your numbers don't have to be exact, but you should try to get them in the ballpark. It's worth looking at actual dates and factoring in additional costs like flights, gas, and accommodation fees as applicable. This will help you get a better sense of the overall cost.

Now You Know | **Adding Price Tags to Your Pins**

If you would like your photos to have a price tag included, then you can do this using the pin's description field.

1. Go the pin description field by hovering over a pin and clicking Edit.

2. Type the price you would like to show in the tag somewhere in the description field. You need to include a currency symbol (currently only U.S. dollar and British pounds are supported) and the price in numbers (for example, $18.75).

3. As soon as you have finished typing, the tag will appear in the top left of the pin.

4. Click Save Pin.

Another reason to get the figures as close to accurate as you can is that other Pinterest users will see them and won't know if you added the price tag or if it came from the original image! You wouldn't want to mislead people. If you are concerned about misleading people, you could explain how you arrived at that cost in the description field. For example, "The price for this vacation was based on a family of four flying from San Francisco in late August."

Let Others Make Their Choices

Once you have done the groundwork in pinning an assortment of realistic choices, you can unleash the board to those you are planning to vacation with. This might be your partner, children, extended family, groups of friends, or all of the above. You can encourage your audience to make comments on pins and enjoy the general discussion around the options. Hopefully, after a short amount of time, the choices that most people like will make themselves apparent. Then might be a good time to repin the chosen elements to a new vacation planning board.

Make a Genealogy Board

Genealogy is a subject that generates much interest today. In recent years many different resources have come online, and you can get plenty of guidance with online research and find many interesting and important family documents without having to leave your home. At the same time, social networks and the general increase in most people's online presence have also helped to bring distant relatives closer together. But while online resources and communities are now aplenty, many people's family history projects still remain offline. This is perhaps because some genealogists are extremely protective of their data, but others simply have collections of old photos and documents that they never got around to doing anything with. However, one thing is clear from our own genealogy research—while you may collect all manner of materials and documents, it's very hard to post anything other than photos in a visually appealing way. Some researchers create their own web sites, which allow the flexibility to share a lot of the fruits of their research online. But even simple web sites require a certain level of technical knowledge to set up and a reasonable amount of time to maintain, and making it easy for others to find your web site remains a challenge. A genealogy Pinterest board, on the other hand, is visual, easy to set up, and easy to search.

One thing to say up front is that the best use of Pinterest in genealogy is as a sharing facility rather than as a primary place to organize your research. With Pinterest it's very difficult to show relationships between things you have pinned. So ideally, you might have an account with a genealogy site such as Ancestry.com or FamilyTreeMaker, where you complete the data-entry part of the work, and then share the in-progress or completed family tree diagram via Pinterest. Another benefit to using applications designed for genealogy is that many of them have a back-up process, meaning you are extremely unlikely to lose your research.

But Pinterest can play an important role in telling your family history, whether the genealogical records you've traced are sitting in boxes and files or already in digital form. The speed of uploading local files to Pinterest makes it a logical choice for getting photos and documents online. Additionally, the ease of pinning directly from web sites gives you a manageable way to harness online resources and add them to your collection.

This section focuses on many things you might consider adding to a genealogy board to create a family history project. It is not only easy and quick to do, but also makes use of content that might otherwise just sit on an archive disc. Instead, you can share your family's story in a way that is visually appealing and that includes links to useful information.

Decide on the Nature of Your Board

One thing to consider before you dive right in is what kind of project you are embarking on and what your desired effect is. If you are looking to simply consolidate all of your family history research in one place, then a single board is a logical way to start. However, if you are looking to have various strands to your genealogy boards, then you might want to plan ahead and decide what you want to put on each board before you start pinning. For instance, you may be researching more than one family and want to keep each one on a separate board. You may want to keep different generations on different boards, or photos on one board and documents on another. It can be helpful (although not essential) to have an idea of how you plan to go about this before you actually start. If you want to dive right in, then that can work too. You can always repin things to different boards as the need arises.

Look for Primary Sources to Pin
================================
Look for Primary Sources to Pin

Primary sources are original materials, documenting something that happened at a given time, and written or produced at that time. Primary sources are the foundation of thorough family research and are needed to establish facts. Good primary sources for genealogy include

- **Census records**   These have been taken every 10 years in the U.S. since 1790 and can be found online. If you are researching other countries, you may find exceptions in the frequency of the census— for example, no census was conducted in the U.K. in 1941.

- **Vital records**   Often referred to as BMD (Birth, Marriage, Death) records in the research community, birth and death certificates and marriage licenses will form a large part of your documentation. They also make attractive visual pins.

- **Military service records**   These can be found in the National Archives, and can be very helpful in gathering information about relatives. Among other things, they can provide you with your ancestor's rank, unit, date mustered in and mustered out, basic biographical information, medical information, and military information.

- **Other documentation**   Things like immigration records, and courthouse and town hall documents like licenses and property deeds can be great pins.

Add Secondary Sources

Secondary sources are documents and records that were not created at the time that an event occurred. Secondary sources are often provided by someone retelling past events, and may not always be completely accurate. However, they can still support primary sources and make great pins for a board. Examples include

- **Family letters and correspondence**   It's definitely worth asking relatives for anything they have in cigar boxes and so forth as these can be real gems for your board. When we embarked on family research, the penmanship alone made these delightful to look at.

- **Family history books**   You may find others have written about your family in the course of their own family research. Pinning such information can help fill some gaps you may have and save you some time.

- **Interviews conducted with relatives**   Many genealogy books and resources will encourage you to conduct interviews with relatives. If relatives are willing to be videotaped, you can pin these interviews to your board.

- **Family trees**   Any family trees you have will make fantastic pins to your board. You will probably find the details are too small to read, but the basic layout of family trees makes them easily identifiable, even when very small.

Make Pins from Online Resources

There is a whole host of excellent family research content on the Internet already—from paid genealogy sites, to public record offices, to obituaries, to personal blogs and web sites. Regardless of the online resources you find directly, you may find the approaches, techniques, and ideas that other researchers have used beneficial to your project. You could use such resources to help get yourself started on tricky issues and benefit directly from the work that others have already put in.

Depending on each site's policy, you may or may not be able to pin these sources. However, if you can, then they can add useful reading material to your largely visual board.

England Genealogy Roots
#Genealogy #England

1 like   5 repins

google.com

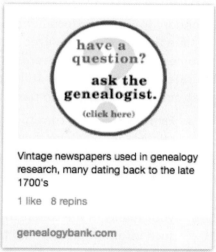

Vintage newspapers used in genealogy research, many dating back to the late 1700's

1 like   8 repins

genealogybank.com

The Coolest Genealogy Charts

3 repins

mytreeandme.com

genealogical tree

1 like   5 repins

heraldikshop.de

Scan and Pin Mementos

In addition to photos and official documents like birth and death certificates, you can pin scanned images or digital photographs of things like maps of family property, family bibles (which were often used to record important events like births and deaths), recipes the family used, military pins and badges, keepsakes, and many other items.

As noted earlier in the chapter, regardless of whether or not you pin these items, it's worth the effort to create digital copies of things that are important to you in case anything happens to the originals.

Allow Other Family Members to Pin

Getting other researchers into your family history to pin to your board will have obvious benefits—you will gain new content from their research and have someone to share the experience with. If you get enough people involved, you may find that the board develops into something like a news bulletin for new research and discoveries. As more and more people join Pinterest, there's also the possibility that you may discover other family members through the site.

Often, the people who do the most genealogical research are older folks, as they are usually the ones with more free time. Pinterest is simple to use, even for people who are not particularly web-savvy. Getting them onto Pinterest might be the easiest way to help them share and present their work.

10

Sharing Boards with Small Groups

While the previous chapters focused on making boards for your own personal usage and large communities, this chapter focuses on boards to share with a select group of people. It's true that all boards are discoverable on Pinterest, but the group boards in this section would typically be made for a group of people you know and interact with on an individual level. The topics and boards we cover in this chapter will assume a certain amount of shared knowledge that only close social groups have, and as such there will be less of a focus on making images and descriptions understandable to unknown readers who happen across the boards through their daily browsing.

In this chapter we first look at using Pinterest boards to help you make selections for a book club. We also look into how to use Pinterest to plan social gatherings in your home and elsewhere—including activities that make your boards truly mobile and leverage the full power of the mobile Pinterest app. You will see that the more your social groups interact with the boards, the stronger and more useful they become—so start getting your friends on Pinterest!

Shortlist Titles for a Book Club

Shortlisting titles for a book club is a fun activity that can often be as enjoyable as reading or discussing the book itself. Lots of formal book clubs use a forum to manage the shortlist discussions. These forums organize conversations into threads, which keep topics combined to certain spaces. If you have an informal book club, like we do, the exchanges tend to take place on an email mailing list or by regular email. Both of these methods work well enough, but do have several problems. First, forums require some kind of moderation to keep threads organized and on topic. Second, forums are generally text-based, which makes it hard to share images. Group email exchanges are just plain unwieldy. People will join the exchanges at various times without reading the latest email the first email. It then becomes almost impossible to know who has said what. All this can make it very hard for the group to arrive at a consensus.

Pinterest overcomes many of the obstacles that group emails and forums present for book club discussions. Given that you will likely shortlist less than dozen titles at a time, everything will be clearly visible in one place. Also, because the board is visual, you will be able to get a great sense of what's on the table straight away—a board of book covers quickly conveys more information than a list of text titles. A Pinterest board will allow you to attach people's comments on each title to each pin. This means you or any book club member can quickly determine which books are most popular rather than having to wait for someone to summarize the email exchanges or forum posts.

Make Sure You Allow All Members of Your Club to Pin

This kind of board could be truly collaborative if you get all of your members onto Pinterest and allow them to pin to this board. When you create the board you should add all of the members' Pinterest user names in the section "Who can pin?"; this will allow them to add book titles or other content to the book club board. These permissions will only apply to this board, so you don't have to worry about them posting to other boards you may have.

Try to Find Pin Sources That Aren't Only Images

In addition to being able to show the book cover on your pin, another great benefit of using Pinterest for shortlisting is that you can create pins that provide more information on the books you're considering. For example, you can pin sources where people can obtain the book, saving everyone some research time. You can also include professional reviews of the books in the pin, making it easier for club members to read about the book before making their comments. To do this, you can pin the book image directly from the review page (if there is an image there), or pin from any source and then edit the pin, pasting the review link in over the source URL.

Another great resource is pinning from your local library. Not only is this source free, but it also will allow you to check availability of the book, the number of copies kept, and whether the library offers a book club set that you can borrow and when that is available.

Add Useful Notes to Your Pins

Make good use of the description field when you create your pins by adding a short description of the book—you can usually find this on purchase sites like Amazon.com or review sites. Remember that if you highlight the text on the page that you want to use for the description, it will automatically be entered as the title of the pin. Once you have your pin and description in place, you can add things like reviews in the comments sections.

Encourage an Exchange of Comments

Once your board is created and some titles for consideration have been pinned, you can all start using the board. Encourage your members to visit each pin and make a comment on each of the titles. It's a good idea to capture positive and negative comments about each title as this will help you narrow down your field. Once people have had the opportunity to comment on the titles, you can start to remove some of the less popular pins. These might include pins that people have read before or titles that just don't appeal. Once you are left with the shortened list, it will be very quick to see which are the most popular by glancing at the length and nature of the comments.

Run a Scavenger Hunt

The scavenger (or treasure) hunt is a big favorite with our family. It's a great way to entertain groups of people and keep young minds active. The big downside to scavenger hunts though is that they can take a lot of preparation. On camping trips we have spent hours wandering the site looking for places to hide clues and to get a sense of what kind of puzzles you can set up for your contestants. Pinterest has proved to be a great way to get a scavenger hunt organized without having to plan too much or even visit the venue (assuming you know it pretty well). The hunt works best if your teams have access to an iPhone or Android smartphone with the Pinterest app installed. You can do it with a basic camera phone with Internet access too, but it's less fluid.

To demonstrate a scavenger hunt on a Pinterest board, we found a great idea online for running such an event at your local mall. Malls work really nicely as venues because contestants are usually familiar with the place, they are big enough to not have every team following each other, they are really easy to set challenges for, and you can take care of getting a prize while the hunt is underway—saving you time and a trip to the mall just for that purpose. One of the great things about the Pinterest scavenger hunt is that it does not require anyone to buy or acquire anything, which would cost contestants money and need to be carried around for the whole hunt. Nor does it require anyone to post clues or tasks around the venue hours in advance (which might get removed or lost). Because it's entirely visual, you can manage virtually everything from your Pinterest board.

Understand the Basic Outline of a Pinterest Scavenger Hunt

The whole methodology of the Pinterest scavenger hunt is to have your hunters working off of a board containing the clues or tasks that you have put together. As they move through the venue, they can look for answers to each clue or task. The clues or tasks should be set in such a way that the answers can be photos taken somewhere in the venue. When the teams find an answer, they can take a photo and pin it to the board (along with team name) and move onto the next clue or task. The team with the most pins at the end of the allotted time wins!

Set Up Your Scavenger Hunt

The first thing you will need to do is to create a Pinterest board for the scavenger hunt. You will need to name the board and grant permission to all participants in the scavenger hunt by entering their names in the section "Who can pin?". (Your participants must first have a Pinterest account and must follow you on Pinterest.) These permissions will allow the participants to pin onto the board you created.

It's also nice to make the board cover into an announcement so that the board is easy to recognize for those looking at your entire board collection. We did this using the Sticky option on Pinstamatic (see Chapter 5 for more information on this). We stated the location and start and end times. We also made a Sticky for the rules of the game.

The Great Mall
Scavenger Hunt
7/27/2012
No pins before
10:00
No pins after
11:30

The place and the rules.

1 like

pinstamatic.com

The next stage is putting up the pins for the tasks. Again, we used Pinstamatic for this because it allows you to type in text and choose a range of fonts and styles to add variety to your board. For the mall hunt, for example, you might like to ask for a store's opening times on a certain day. It's probably best to avoid tasks that involve going into stores and handling merchandise too much as this could easily irritate the staff. It's a good idea to write the tasks out in a text program (like Microsoft Word or Text Pad) and number them. Once you have a full set, you can start pinning them to the board (via Pinstamatic if you wish). It's a good idea to give each task a number, as shown in Figure 10-1, that participants can reference when pinning their photos. You might also like to pin in reverse order if you wish the pins to appear consecutively on the board.

Run the Hunt

You can arrange a gathering point for the start and end of the hunt. Once you have everyone ready to start, it's a good idea to restate the rules of the game. These are basically to take a photo that completes the task and pin it to the board including their team name.

As the teams set off, you will have some minutes to kill as the teams get oriented and familiar with the board. It's a nice opportunity to go and pick up your prize or simply to grab a latte! A few minutes into the

Figure 10-1   *Scavenger hunt clues on Pinterest*

hunt, you will start to see pins appearing on your board. You can then start recording which teams have answered which questions correctly. You will have to do this outside of Pinterest because the boards can't support continually updating text. It's a good idea to keep running totals as you will need to cut the hunt off at the time you agreed and not accept anything pinned after that time. You can comment on the teams' pins on the board if they have not answered correctly. As the teams gather back at the meeting point, you will already have a good idea of the winner!

Run the Hunt Without a Smartphone

As we said earlier, this option is not as fluid, but the hunt can still be run provided people have an Internet browser on their phone and picture messaging enabled. The participants should use the browser to see the board and the pins as outlined before. They would also take photos as before, but obviously not using the Pinterest app. Instead of pinning their images to the board, they can message them to you. If you wish, you can pin them to the board, or you can simply just make notes of which questions have been answered by which team.

Create an Exercise Regimen

You can use a Pinterest board to plan out a customized exercise regimen that you can access and update with new exercises and tips as your needs and focus change. One of the difficulties in planning a regimen is that you may not know exactly what an exercise is designed to do and what combinations are good. Using a Pinterest board, you can gather visuals and quick links to more descriptive web sites explaining all you need to know about each exercise. These sources can also give you sound advice about the exercise, what sort of numbers to aim for (in terms of repetitions or distance), and generally how to get the most out of the exercise.

It can also be fun to share your regimen with others and encourage them to participate and share their own ideas. If you work out with a partner or group, everyone can share his or her progress and offer collective encouragement by pinning and adding comments to the board. Your Pinterest exercise board can also function as a social calendar for group exercising. You can use it to pin plans and locations for meet-ups and links to things like maps, directions, and general information about the places on your calendar.

Plan a Home Exercise Regimen for You and Others

The Internet is full of articles, how-to pages, videos, and diagrams for different exercises and programs. A good starting point is to focus on what you want the core elements of your regimen to be—for example, cardio workouts or toning and strengthening particular body areas.

For our group regimen, we decided to focus on abs and cardio, shown in Figure 10-2, as this was what most people planning to participate wanted. We found a video online for exactly the kind of regimen we wanted to follow. Online videos of this nature are good resources and can be comparable to some commercial DVDs that cost a fair amount of money. However, you might find (as we did) that the videos run you through the workout in real time, but don't offer you any real instruction or guidance on how to ensure you are doing the exercises properly. This is the point when your board becomes truly useful! For each individual exercise or activity, you can find and pin helpful supplementary information, such as step-by-step instructions,

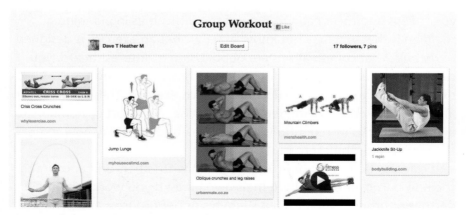

Figure 10-2   *A group exercise plan*

diagrams showing which muscles the exercise targets, and ways to make sure you're doing the exercise correctly.

The other members of your group should be allowed to pin useful resources they have found too. It might also be fun to encourage some sharing of comments on the pins. For example, if someone is finding a particular exercise tough, members of the group could offer some encouragement and support, or generally share in their pain. In this sense, the social nature of the board can be a real strength as it unites the group in a common shared goal.

Plan an Outside Group Exercise Regimen

The second way to use Pinterest for group exercise that we have explored is using your board as a social calendar to plan exercise meet-ups for your group. It is well-known that adding a group or social context to exercising makes it more enjoyable, and therefore more likely you'll stick with it.

As long as you have a group of people who want to work out together and you can find enough mutually acceptable time windows, then a daily group exercise board can work. This might be a group of work colleagues exercising on a lunch break, or even a group of students working out between classes. The scenario we used when we created our board was a group of mothers who have a certain window of free time each day to devote to exercise.

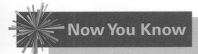

Now You Know **Using Image Search Engines to Find Good Pins**

When you have a particular type of picture you want to display use the image search feature that most major search engines have. First do a regular web search. When you see the web results, look for the "images" option (sometimes this appears among the web results with a row of the top images for that search). Going to the image search results page will show you only images. When you click the image, you'll go to the source page for the image and can pin from there.

It might be helpful to start out by defining the times that everyone can make. You can then start making a list of activities that can be done in your local area, are good sources of exercise, and provide a social opportunity. It might also be fun to think of things that some people had not tried before or would be willing to try if they were part of a group. Once the activities and possible locations have been decided, you can start looking for good sources of pins. It's sometimes good to pin from an official web site that provides useful resources such as opening hours, maps, and any prices that might apply. Even if the site doesn't have good images, the usefulness of the information makes pinning from it worthwhile.

Once you have decided on your full list of activities and sources, you can begin scheduling the activities and pinning them to the board, using the description box to state the day each activity was planned for, the location, and the activity itself. Remember to pin them in reverse order if you want the pins to appear in chronological order. Once everything looks the way you want it, you are ready to share the board with the group.

Build a Wish List

There are plenty of occasions to build wish lists—birthdays, Christmas, weddings, moving away to college, and so on. Though sometimes these seem self-indulgent, they do make it easier for those who want to buy gifts for the occasion. In the past we've made wish lists by email or by using a shopping site (like Amazon), but these have their limitations. Email wish lists don't allow for easy communication between those who are buying—you often end up with a confusing thread of who is getting what, what isn't available right now, and who doesn't have the right store near them. Shopping sites, on the other hand, allow you to centralize the list and allow users to see what has already been purchased, but it limits the list to items carried by that vendor. It's also pretty rare that a commerce site like Amazon will always have the best price, so it may end up costing friends and family more than necessary. Gift registries have the same problems as shopping sites. It also seems odd that you would want all of your gifts from the same place—what if you like the bedding from Nordstrom but the crockery from Macy's? The benefits of a well-developed registry service are pretty obvious for the seller but they leverage the ease and simplicity to limit the customer to their own goods.

In this section we'll show you how to use Pinterest to make a wish list that is easy to access, allows communication with all those buying gifts, and allows the creator to keep the costs down as much as possible.

Decide Who and What

The first thing to make clear is who the list is for and what it is for. Other Pinterest users may see your board or pins and like or repin things, but it's unlikely they will seek the board out and plaster it with comments. To help ensure this is the case, try to be as explicit as possible when naming your board. Try including the recipient's name and the event. Avoid "Wedding Wish List" in favor of "James Smith and Mary Jones' Wedding Gift Registry."

Use a Variety of Sources

One of the key benefits of using Pinterest over a shopping site is that you can include items from multiple sellers. That means you can pin the exact item you want. If the item is only available from one site, then you can still request it. If you like pants from Old Navy, but T-shirts from Hollister—no problem! You can pin both.

The second key benefit is that you can shop around for those who are buying for you. In our experience people often interpret wish lists incorrectly, thinking you *have to* buy that exact item. Often gift-buyers will pay a higher price just to ensure they get it exactly right. Our kids' grandparents once purchased a train set on Amazon for 30 percent more than it would have cost from a local big box store because they weren't sure and didn't want to get it wrong. Of course, sometimes the opposite is also true—you do want *that* specific Blu-ray disc with the special anniversary director's commentary. Either way, researching it yourself and using Pinterest to present the list helps rule out these confusions.

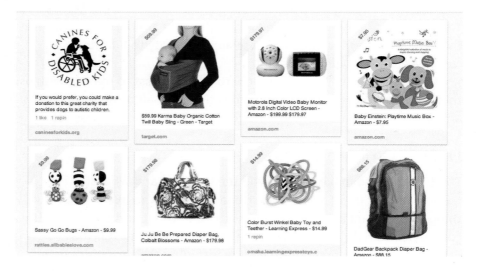

Allow for Charity

Charitable donations in lieu of physical gifts are very popular, especially for weddings of couples who already have all the bedding and kitchen utensils they need. If you have a charity you would like people to donate to instead of buying a gift, you can pin something about this, such as a link to the charity's web site. This is a nice feature to add to any wish list as it allows the buyer to be anonymous in the amount they want to spend and helps charities to continue the great work they do for worthy causes.

Now You Know — Understand Why Images Sometimes Don't Appear in the Pin Box

Sometimes you will try to pin something but the image you want won't appear in the available selection. In many cases this is because of the way that web site is built and the technology it uses. Most often it is because the web site is using Adobe Flash—a multimedia platform that adds interactivity to a web site (such as images that change when you hover your cursor on them, animations, and image slideshows). Pinterest cannot pin images that are in Flash. One way around this is to right-click the image and click Copy Image Location. You can then upload a pin using the copied text. Alternatively, you can take a screenshot, crop the image, save it and pin it to your board from your computer.

Use Price Tags and Text from the Page

It's really helpful for your buyers to see the price ranges of the gifts you are asking for. You can provide this information by adding price labels to each of your pins. Simply make sure that the description text contains the price and currency symbol (for example, $15.00) and that price will appear on the pin in the top-left corner of the image, as shown in the previous illustration.

Get the Most Out of the Description Field

Be sure to make the information in the description field as specific as you can. If you want an item in a particular size, then state that here. If you want a particular color and there isn't an image of the item in that color, then say so in the description field. It's also useful to indicate the source of the pin in the description. Maybe some people who are buying gifts already have accounts set up at certain vendors and can make purchases there easily. Maybe they are planning a purchase from that vendor and can consolidate their purchases for a discount or free shipping. You might also want to use the description field to state that the item is also available from other sellers, including local rather than online vendors.

You'll find that it can be pretty time-consuming to keep typing out descriptions and prices for each pin. You can avoid this by simply highlighting the text you want to use in the description (for example, the product name and price) before clicking the Pin It button. This will copy the selected text to the description field as soon as you select your image.

Encourage People to Use the Comments Field

Wish lists on shopping sites will let you know what has been purchased and what hasn't. Pinterest will not do this, so you'll need to rely on those buying gifts to update the comments on each pin when they make a purchase. This will help avoid duplicate gifts. You might also like to ask buyers to use the comment field on each pin to discuss the item rather than in an email as all comments are attached to the item in question. You could also use the comment field to post links to online coupons you find or upcoming special offers that you notice that might benefit the buyer. If someone is having a gift sent directly to you, it would be very useful to have them post the tracking number in the comment field too, so you know when to expect delivery.

Plan a Dinner Party

We love to cook and love to host dinner parties. It's a lot of hard work, but the enjoyment of eating good food with good friends and not having to hire a sitter to watch the kids can far outweigh the stress of putting a dinner party together. Perhaps the hardest thing about hosting a dinner party is the food, and it's easy to get fixated on that—what to cook, when to prep everything, when to start cooking things, and so forth. But then we find that we forget all of the other preparations for the party—table settings, napkins folding, a seating plan.

Well thank goodness for Pinterest! Using a Pinterest board to plan your dinner party allows you to start with a blank canvas, gradually adding and deleting, pinning reminders, and shaping things until you achieve exactly the kind of party you want.

Plan and Share the Menu

Sharing the menu in advance with your guests can be great fun! It's almost like looking at a menu before you go to a restaurant. To do this, of course, you need to plan the menu well ahead of time, preferably when you have an empty board. We let ourselves go a little crazy and pin all sorts of things to our boards. When a board has only food and recipes on it, we find it much easier to visualize the entire meal. Sometimes we notice themes within the food choices, flavors that complement each other, and ingredients that are out of season or hard to get, or even beyond the budget we have set ourselves. Gradually, we start deleting pins until we are left with the menu we are going to go with. This whole process can take days and even weeks, depending on how much you start with and how much time you can dedicate to the process. If, like us, you keep changing your mind, then it can take even longer!

We prefer to pin from recipe web sites, even when we know the recipe we want to use or have it in a cookbook. We find pinning the recipe to our board acts as a visual reminder for when the time comes to shop for ingredients. You might also like to add notes to your pins that you can use while deciding on the final menu—is something particularly tricky to make? Is the dessert very labor-intensive and likely to take you away from your guests for too long? Did you see or try this recipe before? All of these things can be helpful as you shape your menu. When you have it ready, you can share it with your guests—this will also be an opportunity for any guests to let you know if there is something planned that they can't eat (see Figure 10-3).

Shop for the Things You Need

Shopping for the things you will need for the dinner party is crucial. It's one aspect where a little planning goes a long way. We try to think of places we'll need to go for special items like wine and cheeses and pin

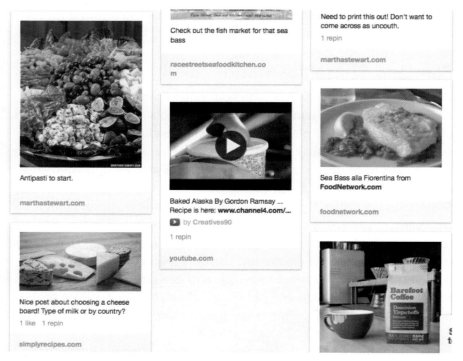

Figure 10-3 *A dinner party menu*

those places to our board. If you like to shop locally at farmers' markets or specialty stores, these places are not always open every day and sometimes require a dedicated errand. These visual reminders help us to think about how we are going to tackle the shopping efficiently.

Plan Place Settings and Table Décor

As we said before, the food and shopping can sometimes take over with dinner parties and whatever you were going to do about the music, place settings, and decorating for the party gets forgotten. If you start pinning these things onto your Pinterest board, you will likely start thinking about them sooner. You'll soon realize if you are missing something you need and can add that to your shopping list. For example, we added a link to a site showing the napkin folding we wanted to do—each time we saw it, it was a reminder to practice. We had it down in no time and on the evening of the party we were able to fold the napkins in less than three minutes! Think about what you need for your place settings, what kind of look you want to create, the candles you want in the centerpiece (if any). When you know what you want and have it all to hand, the assembly takes no time at all.

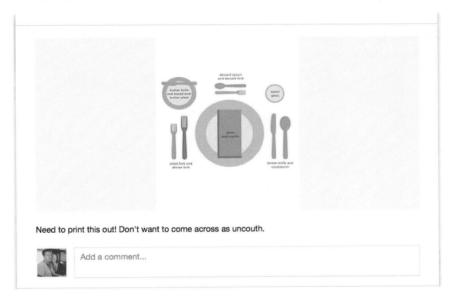

Need to print this out! Don't want to come across as uncouth.

Add a comment...

Plan Entertainment

Providing a little ambiance and some kind of after-dinner entertainment can be very useful to have planned and they can add a little visual variety to your board. You might like to think about what music to play so you can build a playlist (this can also be a reminder to move the iPod dock or CD player to wherever it needs to be) or what games to play after dinner if your friends are into that. We always like to have a few old board games ready in case anyone feels like playing.

Share Your Plans with Guests

It's a lot of fun to share your board with your guests before the party—a nice little preview of the evening to come. I like to put the board link into an Evite (evite.com; other online invitation sites are also available). You might even like to have guests comment or vote on the menu items if you can't decide what to make or are unsure of particular diets or dislikes among your guests. The board itself will make a lovely memento of the evening long after everyone has gone and the dishes have been done.

11

Use Boards to Raise Awareness of Issues and Events

In recent years, organizations have really embraced social media, such as Facebook and Twitter, to extend their reach to a wider online audience. As Pinterest establishes itself in the social media space, more and more organizations are turning to this network as a major part of their online presence.

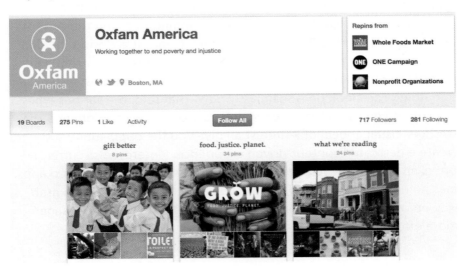

So if major organizations are starting to use Pinterest to promote things and raise awareness, why shouldn't you? Throughout this chapter we will look at ways you can use Pinterest to promote events, how you can highlight crucial details, drive traffic to your sponsors, and document previous years' efforts. We also look at using boards to build up awareness of certain topics of interest to you, with the aim of increasing awareness. We will see how Pinterest boards can be created simply and easily for small events with a niche audience, to grand, large-scale life events like weddings. This chapter aims at giving you everything you need to promote whatever you choose, by building creative and engaging boards that give your audience upfront details and an overall visual impression of the event or topic.

Promote a Local Event

Local events, such as festivals, yard sales, school functions, and fundraisers are part and parcel of our lives.

If you have an event to promote, Pinterest could prove to be an excellent way to get it the wide public exposure it needs.

There are, of course, limitations to Pinterest, but then that is true of any web site you might choose to use. The big drawback to Pinterest is that, as of this writing, the number of community members is small compared to sites like Facebook. This is changing fast, and the current level of growth of the Pinterest community means it is closing the gap on Facebook, but there is still a big gap to close. It is also currently not possible to put an event into an online calendar via Pinterest—something Facebook does seamlessly now. That said, the various types of content you can pin, the speed and ease of board creation, and the stronger visual appeal of Pinterest all give you the opportunity to create a dedicated content-driven experience. Pinterest also currently offers an experience relatively free of distractions (like integrated apps, messaging, and advertising), giving you a better opportunity to grab viewers' attention and communicate the essentials of your message more effectively.

Share the Key Details

Another partial limitation of Pinterest is the fact that pins cannot be reordered, but this can be overcome with a little planning—when making an events board, it's essential to decide what you want at the top of the board before you start. You should then pin the most important things last.

As with any event, the what, where, when, why, and how are crucial pieces of information. For this reason, we'd recommend including all of these things in the board description field so it's the first thing someone sees when they open the board. We'd also recommend pinning these last, so they sit neatly on the top row of your board.

The What   It's very important to find or create a pin that can quickly and effectively communicate what your event is about. You may accomplish this in finer detail with various pins later down on the board, but your "top row" pins (including their description fields) are your chance to grab the viewers' attention. Sometimes logos and posters can do this effectively; other times photos of the event can help.

The Where   Pinning an image of a map will help people know immediately whether attending is a possibility for them. Try creating a Google/Yahoo!/Mapquest map with the exact location highlighted, and pin a screenshot of that page. Alternatively, you could use Pinstamatic to pin the location directly without having to bother with screenshots.

The When   For our board on a local beer and music festival, we chose to use the calendar pin function of Pinstamatic. The function shows the date(s) clearly in the image and you can clarify using the description field.

The Why   Sometimes the cause will be the most compelling reason for people to attend. If your event is in support of a charitable cause or social concern, then you might like to pin some information related to this in a prominent position—perhaps the logos of local charities or organizations that benefit.

The How   In the case of the festival we promoted, the event was ticketed, so it was important to pin information on how to get tickets and how much they cost. Depending on your event, this may or may not be relevant, but it could be helpful to see any information related to expectations (admission prices, directions, parking, etc.). If there is a cost involved, remember to include the currency and price in the description field to make the price label show on the pin.

Give Examples of What Is on Show

Presumably your event is *about* something, so you should consider pinning some examples of what people could expect to see at the event. If a person or group is performing at your event, even if they are relatively unknown outside of your local community, then you could pin something about them, perhaps from any web sites they may have including Facebook or MySpace pages. If people are exhibiting things, try pinning something about what they're showing. Our board is about a beer and music festival, so we made pins for different breweries and showcase beers that would be on sale. We also made pins for the bands performing at the festival. We were very fortunate to have one band of international fame performing, so it was pretty easy to pin content about them and we used the Spotify pin functionality on Pinstamatic to pin links to tracks they were known for. For another band, we pinned directly from their web site, and for a group really only known within the city, we pinned their Facebook page.

Pin Photos of Previous Events

Photos and videos from previous events make excellent pins (if this is not the first time the event has been held). These photos and videos can convey, more than anything else, the real flavor of the event. If you aren't able to find anything online, it's definitely worth asking around to see if someone can send you photos to upload.

Link to Other Social Media

If your event has a site dedicated to it aside from Pinterest, then offering links here will allow readers to follow your event on Twitter, Facebook, or any service that your event is using. Depending on the restrictions of the sites you are using, you'll need to use the workaround we outlined in "Point People to Other Places They Can Find You" in Chapter 9 to create these kinds of pins. In the case of Facebook, you cannot pin directly from their domain, and in the case of Twitter, there are sometimes no images to pin and other times it's only the profile image (which doesn't tell the reader immediately that it's a Twitter handle).

For both of these sites, we have gotten into the habit of keeping Twitter and Facebook icons in our images folders to upload manually—we can then edit those pins, adding in the URL to the Twitter or Facebook feed or page.

Highlight Your Sponsors

Depending on the scale and cost of your event, you may have sponsors who help make it happen. Keeping sponsors happy and motivated to continue their support is crucial to the event's funding. With this in mind, making space on your board for links to any sponsor is a nice way to try and send some traffic or business their way. It can serve as an example of how much you appreciate their support and are committed to give them extra exposure.

Pinterest is very effective for small business referrals—Pinterest users are 79 percent more likely to purchase items they saw pinned to Pinterest boards versus what Facebook users see on their newsfeeds, according to a recent survey from online behavioral commerce platform SteelHouse. If the organizations sponsoring your event are small local businesses, then there's a real possibility of them finding customers through this exposure. It's also worth checking if these businesses have Pinterest boards, so you can repin examples of whatever service they provide, and encourage them to pin items about your event as well.

Planning an Event

Planning events on Pinterest is very popular indeed; people really seem to love sharing and repinning their ideas for all kinds of parties, receptions, and more. For our sample boards, we chose to plan two types of events—a themed birthday party and a wedding—because they demonstrate the full extent to which you can use Pinterest in your event planning. You could easily use the ideas we outline here for a graduation or retirement party, a bar mitzvah, a Super Bowl party—anything!

As with many of the projects we've already presented in the book, our boards evolved from conceptual boards, where we initially dumped lots of ideas, into refined visualizations of how we wanted the actual event to be. In each case, we started by pinning everything we liked and then gradually scaled that back to what we really wanted and were going to do. For our boards, the desired end-state was a board we could share as a little preview with the guests. We thought it would be fun and a little something different to add the preview board to the invitations.

Let People Know the Location

Every party needs a venue—it might be your home in the case of a birthday party, or an outside venue in the case of a wedding. Whether you are partying at home or away, it's nice to show the location—at the very least it'll provide those with whom you share the board the sense of where they will be. And if your venue is not your home, pinning the venue allows guests to check it out in advance. You can pin from the venue's official home page, but you should also consider pinning from third-party sites like TripAdvisor or Yelp to provide sources for independent opinions. If your event requires guests to stay overnight, it's also nice to indicate recommended places nearby so people can make arrangements to find lodgings.

Create Pins for Clothing

For certain events clothing will obviously be more important than for others. On a wedding board, you'll want pins dedicated to what the bride, bridal party, groom, and groomsmen will all be wearing. Seeing these things side by side on a Pinterest board is a great way to assess how everything will look together and serves as a nice reference for coordinating flowers, the cake, and many other components of the wedding. With a themed birthday party, costume ideas are a nice thing to pin for parents who will need to put one together. It also reinforces the idea that costumes are a part of the party for anyone that didn't notice that.

For other events, clothing may well be a small part of the event. Graduations often require the renting of a gown, religious ceremonies have their own particular clothing, and family reunions often feature an event t-shirt—these would all make great pins for your board. And maybe you are just buying an outfit specifically for this event, in which case you might want to use a pin from a site like Polyvore to share your ideas.

Think About Invitations and Thank-Yous

While you may still want to send email invitations like an Evite or traditional paper invitations in the mail, it's also nice to include an invitation on your board that covers the basics of the event. In fact, why not make an invitation the board cover? The cover is a way to summarize the board as a whole and an invitation or statement of the

Look out for your invitations!

papermints.com

Mark the date people!

Uploaded by user

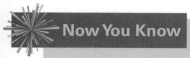

Making an Invitation into a Board Cover

Typically, your invitation will exist only in non-digital form, so your first step will be to make it digital. You can do this by scanning it or photographing it—although using a camera may cause the text to be unreadable due to flash reflections. If there is a copy of your invitation online, you could take a screenshot of it and save that file to your computer, then upload it and set it as your board cover. To take a screenshot:

1. Go to the page your image is on.

2. On a PC: Press the CTRL-PRT SCN.

   On a Mac: Press COMMAND-SHIFT-4 and drag the crosshairs icon to cover the area you want captured.

3. On a PC: Open an image editing application (like Microsoft Paint) and paste the image there. Save the file to your computer.

   On a Mac: Once you have dragged the crosshairs and released the mouse, the image is sent directly to your desktop.

most important information (what, when, where, and why) is a great way to frame the content. For the wedding board, we made a "save the date" announcement the board cover. If you are doing formal invitations and, later, formal thank you cards, then you can pin these to your board too. They can be both reminders to place the orders for the items, and a great way to see if your themes or colors are consistent throughout the board.

Give People an Idea of the Menu

Food and drink are among the most popular things to pin throughout Pinterest, so you can definitely browse other people's boards for cool ideas to repin to your board in addition to finding things yourself elsewhere on the Internet. If you are planning to prepare the food yourself, pinning your food ideas to your event board has a number of benefits. First, you can quickly see if your menu is balanced the way you want it. Do you have too many sweet items? Do you want more healthy options? Do you have food items that are too similar? All of these questions will be easy to answer once you see everything in front of you on your board. Second, when it comes to buying your ingredients, you will have all of your recipes in one place and not in a long list of bookmarks—this will make your shopping list easier to compile. Finally, you'll also be able to pin ideas and recipes that worked well to another board for another event.

If you intend to have someone cater the event for you, you could use your board as a place to collect ideas or dishes you would like for your event. You could then show your caterer the board to give them a sense of what you are looking for. If you have decided on your caterer, you could pin things from their web site or catalog to your board and give their business a little free advertising.

Most events require some kind of cake, and this is a great thing to pin. You can try searching within Pinterest for cake ideas—there are thousands! If you have chosen what you want, you can pin an image of that.

Consider How You Want to Handle Gifts

For a wedding, a birthday party, or most kinds of events, you will want the board to be about the venue, the food, and most importantly the event itself rather than it being a list of gifts you want. That said, for most events we attend or host, people always ask about what kind of gifts to buy. One happy medium here is to build a wish list and pin the list as one item in your board. Refer back to "Build a Wish List" in Chapter 10 for lots of good ideas on this, including registries for charities.

Document the Real Event

Don't forget to update your board with photos of the actual event (and allow your guests to do this also). The combination of planning pins and photos of the actual event will make your event board into a unique scrapbook-like memento of the event in all its splendor!

Raise Awareness of a Topic

Using Pinterest to raise awareness of a topic you care about is a natural extension of its general usage. In a sense, the board you create becomes a topic page, with you vetting and updating the best content to pin to it. Once you start making this kind of board, you will see that it functions on two levels—it shares relevant content with people who share your interest in the topic, but can also be used to bookmark things you either want to read later or revisit at some point.

As our example here, we have a board dedicated to the topic of microfinance (the process of making small loans from one individual to another, typically in the developing world via a microloan company), something we are deeply interested in. But really, given the pliability of Pinterest, you really can mold it to any topic you like—from a particular health condition, to animal welfare, to a local ballot proposition, to an academic topic, or even an environmental issue.

Point People Toward the Best Sites

The true value of the Pinterest topic board is that you as the board's creator can determine the content. You can perform the job of curating and highlighting the best content, filtering the Internet's coverage of the topic in a way that web search and news hub pages can't.

With this in mind, a good place to start is by making pins for the most reliable and authoritative sites. This differs from one-off articles in the sense that these kinds of sources provide consistently relevant content, rather than featuring it from time to time. For example, on our microfinance board, we made sure to include links to the three major loans facilitators, which offer large amounts of high quality content.

Doing this allows users looking at your board to know immediately what the best sources are and to get right into them.

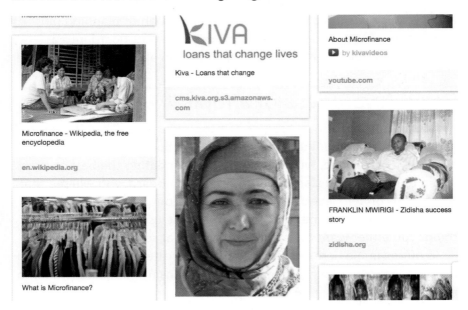

Use Infographics to Communicate Ideas

It doesn't take much browsing to begin noticing infographics on Pinterest. Infographics are visual representations of information, and usually allow you to comprehend complex ideas and processes through an image, rather than by having to read large amounts of text.

They are especially useful for your topic board for a couple of reasons. First, because they are usually very appealing visually, lots of people will view them and often repin them. Second, they give readers of your board a quick understanding of some core piece of information related to your topic, making it accessible to those who may only have a passing interest.

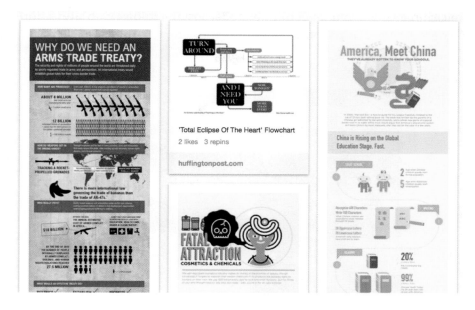

Infographics can sometimes be hard to find online because they are not always labeled that well. You can have some success using images searches, but we found most of ours in the course of reading articles online—typically, many of the trendy technology blogs (like Mashable and TechCrunch) and social sharing sites (like Digg and Tumblr) have plenty of infographics.

Highlight the Important People

Sometimes the people associated with a topic or cause are instantly recognizable and immediately synonymous with the issue. This makes them strong candidates for pins on your board as they can draw in readers who like that particular individual and may be interested in following your board. For example, we pinned Bob Geldof to the microfinance board. He is mostly known (and greatly admired) for his support for fighting poverty in Africa—most notably his Live Aid work. However, most people don't know that he is a champion of microfinance and a patron of one the largest microloan web sites—here Pinterest allows us to connect the dots for people.

Bob Geldof - Patron of the Microloan Foundation.

Muhammad Yunus On Microfinance

forbes.com

In other cases, the important people may not be well known, but you may think they should be! In these cases, you can use your Pinterest board to promote them to the world. We wanted to try and raise the profile of Muhammad Yunus, the man who really developed the concepts of microloans and microcredit. He is quite an outstanding man and someone we think everyone should know about.

Pin Media Mentions

Aside from picking out top quality sites for your readers to have ready access to, you may also like to use your board to pin recent articles of interest related to your topic. This will keep your board fresh and constantly updated with new and engaging pins.

You could also consider using the board as a way of bookmarking articles you want to read later on—simply pin the article to your board whenever you don't have time to read it. Remember, you can always delete the pins later if you determine the article isn't a useful addition to the board. The net result of this is that your board becomes a repository for great articles, images, and videos that would have otherwise been lost.

Support a Cause

So, now that we've considered using Pinterest to raise awareness of a topic, here we look at how you might like to extend this idea to directly support a cause you believe in. When supporting a cause, the topic details themselves are pinned more as background information, providing the basis for the philanthropic nature of the board. For example, you might want to have a board about poverty in Africa that is largely informative on the topic—but *supporting* the cause of *fighting poverty* in Africa would require you to focus more specifically on charities and groups working in that area, and raising awareness of their work.

This section will focus on both building a board to support a cause and ways to reuse some of your previous topic boards to create the message you want to share. We will look at how to plan out your board, give ideas for offering background information, add real life context, and offer people the information they need to support your cause.

Determine the Focus of Your Board

As with all boards built for a specific purpose or topic, a little forward planning will stand you in good stead. It's not absolutely essential, because you can take inspiration from one pin to form the basis of another board. However, if you are approaching Pinterest set on the idea of using it to generate support for a cause, taking a step back for a moment will likely help you to focus on what you want to achieve and how best to go about that—the net result should be a board that speaks to its readers immediately and communicates the message you want to send.

Many people on Pinterest have what you might call general philanthropy boards. These are boards where they pin the charities and organizations that they like and want to show support for. These kinds of boards can be very attractive and interesting to look at, and generally Pinterest users are keen to repin charity and good cause links.

In our opinion, the downside to these boards is that they don't allow you to expand on the topic very much. Because you cannot reorder pins, it quickly becomes difficult to integrate content related to a previous pin. This makes any progression of the board (beyond adding more similar pins) nigh on impossible. But if you know this kind of "directory" experience is what you want to create, then you can jump right in and pin away.

If your intent is to make a board dedicated explicitly to one cause, where you add new content on a regular basis, then it's wise to do a little planning. You need to consider all of the elements you want to include so that in the enthusiasm for pinning, you don't forget anything. You also should think about any sets of pins you want to be grouped, as those items need to be pinned in consecutive order. With a board that is continually being added to, it isn't possible to preserve any positions, so keeping things close together is the best you can do.

Outline the Cause

When working on a specific cause board, you could think about making sure your readers have the basics they need to understand the cause. In order to accomplish this, try looking at the "Raise Awareness of a Topic" section earlier in this chapter, as this covers key areas you might want to mention. Things you will definitely want to think about are

- Infographics that succinctly show readers what the cause is and why it is important. These will allow the readers to familiarize themselves quickly with the topic.

- Who the key organizations and individuals supporting this cause are. These types of pins will be helpful to people who are familiar with the organizations and people but not have connected them to the cause. For example, we donated to and bought from Goodwill Industries for years and were very aware of the organization's existence and presence. It was after only a year or so we realized they supported getting people trained and back into work—a wonderful cause indeed.

- Recent examples of this cause in the media. These can help to jog readers' memories and remind them of things they had heard but forgotten.

Pin Around an Event

An event supporting your cause can be a very positive way to generate support for it. In our Ride a Wave board, we wanted to showcase the work that this group does week in and week out—giving kids with disabilities the chance to experience surfing and kayaking. In this case, we felt showcasing a day with this group was a great way to get people to appreciate the work they do because it made the cause more real.

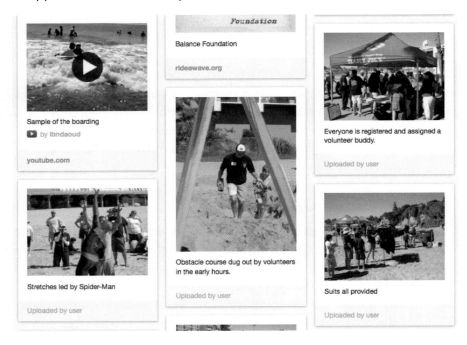

Sample of the boarding
▶ by lbndaoud

youtube.com

Foundation

Balance Foundation

rideawave.org

Everyone is registered and assigned a volunteer buddy.

Uploaded by user

Stretches led by Spider-Man

Uploaded by user

Obstacle course dug out by volunteers in the early hours.

Uploaded by user

Suits all provided

Uploaded by user

Pinning examples of an event can be a lot of work as it requires a certain amount of gathering of material first hand, or at least contacting people who attended for their images and videos. However, it can really be worth the effort because this type of content communicates so much more than pins of logos and links to photo galleries.

Documenting an event supporting your cause can also be done if you didn't attend or know anyone who attended, providing you can access the photos and videos online somewhere. If your cause is a humanitarian effort overseas, you can probably find event-based content within the charity's web site, or even write to the organization asking for access to images and videos.

Look for the Human Angle

Most causes seek to improve the lives of people in some way, be it individuals, groups, or communities. Presenting this human angle can make the cause tangible for people reading, making it resonate strongly. For example, we supported a charity in the U.K. that provided Christmas boxes to children in orphanages in Eastern Europe. While undoubtedly a worthy cause, it was actually seeing video of the children's reaction that really persuaded us to participate.

Sometimes a human angle might show how the organizations fighting the cause have made a difference or bluntly state how serious a problem is—but what works especially well is when you can combine both of these elements. This can help demonstrate clearly how supporting your cause is making a difference to people's lives. Good candidate pins for showing a human angle are case studies that focus on one individual specifically and any news reports or documentaries that showcase an example of the cause.

Use Quotes to Inspire People

Quotes can be an excellent addition to your cause board for many reasons. Perhaps the most obvious reason is that quotes can capture large complicated topics and situations and distill them into an instantly digestible amount of text. You will probably be familiar with pull quotes in printed (and online) material—quotes that are pulled out of the article and put in a larger, more distinct font. These allow the publisher to draw the reader's attention to key messages in the article. Carefully selected quotes can bring simplicity to your message that will stay with your readers and perhaps inspire them.

Unfortunately, quotes often get neglected on Pinterest boards because it's not always obvious how to pin them unless they are embedded into an image. We have seen a great many pins where people resort to leaving the quote in the description field, which is a shame because sometimes you'll want it to be the main focus of your pin. If you do find a quote you want to pin, the best way to do it is to use one of two third-party services—Pinstamatic or Shareasimage.

Both of these sites will help you to convert your text into image pins for your board (see "Making Pins From Non-Images" in Chapter 5 for more details).

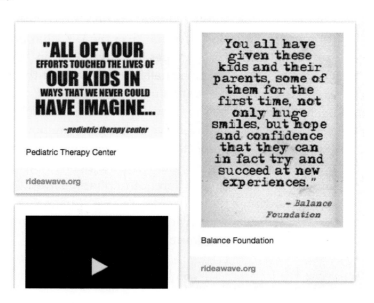

Look for Things Other Supporters Have Pinned

Unless your cause is very specific, there will doubtless be other Pinterest users pinning on the same topic, so you could take a look at what they have already shared on the topic. There are several ways to do this, the most obvious being using the Pinterest search facility. However, Pinterest's search capabilities are currently very basic, especially for those of us more used to the super-complex personalized algorithms of web search—it works only off of text matches and does not allow any filtering of the given results by key pivot points, such as popularity. It does, however, allow for you to filter by pin, person, or board, which can help to narrow down your results.

A lesser known, but incredibly powerful way to search Pinterest is by source. You can run this search easily to show what has been pinned from any top-level domain. This means that if you have a favorite web site for content regarding your cause, you can perform a simple source

Combining Images and Text into One Pin

If you cannot decide if you want your pin to be text (like a quote) or an image, you could consider the option of adding the text into the image. This is most easily achieved using web sites that allow you to create image macros. The term *image macro* is a photo onto which text has been superimposed—think Lolcats and I Can Has Cheeseburger. Although these are typically used for creating funny pictures, there's no reason why you can't use them to create something serious. The steps are simple:

1. Save your image to your computer.

2. Go to your chosen image macro site (for example, http://icanhas.cheezburger.com/) and upload your image.

3. Use the site's editing software to design and place your text.

4. Find your newly created image on the image macro web site. (Lolcats will send you the link in an email.)

5. Pin the image to your board.

6. Edit the destination URL in the pin, so that it goes somewhere related to the image and quote, rather than to the image macro site.

search within Pinterest to see what has already been pinned from that domain. To do this, go to http://pinterest.com/source/*YourWebsite.com*/, replacing *YourWebsite.com* with the web site you wish to search—for example, http://pinterest.com/source/mashable.com/ will show you all pins pinned from Mashable.com.

Help People Get Involved and Donating

As the main focus of your board is supporting a cause or issue, getting people involved is one of the key objectives. In many ways, everything you have pinned previously is leading up to this—you have grabbed the reader's attention and now you want to seize the moment to ask for their support. For that reason, it's important to keep any pins related to getting involved near the top of the page and clearly labeled. If you are supporting a cause that has organizations and charities behind it, then you should be able to use their site to pin something about getting involved. You can try looking for any sub-pages they may have on that topic—Ride a Wave had a whole subsection on this topic that we pinned at the top of our board.

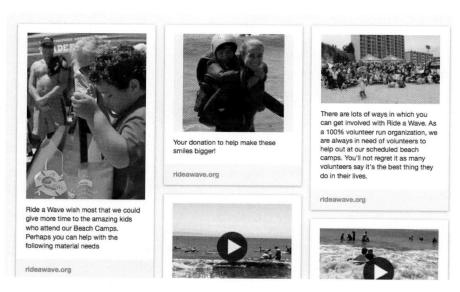

Ride a Wave wish most that we could give more time to the amazing kids who attend our Beach Camps. Perhaps you can help with the following material needs

rideawave.org

Your donation to help make these smiles bigger!

rideawave.org

There are lots of ways in which you can get involved with Ride a Wave. As a 100% volunteer run organization, we are always in need of volunteers to help out at our scheduled beach camps. You'll not regret it as many volunteers say it's the best thing they do in their lives.

rideawave.org

It is equally important to include within your board a clear and obvious way to donate to charities fighting for the cause. The easiest way to do this is to pin the charities' donation pages, making it clear in the description that this is where you can donate. You could also get a little more creative with your donation pins. If you have a photo showing how donations have helped directly, you could pin this, then edit the pin, pasting the actual donation link there. You might also consider creating a text pin using Pinstamatic or Shareasimage—this would work nicely if you want to outline exactly what a certain donation amount could help achieve.

12

Learn About Commercial Uses for Pinterest

As mentioned in Chapter 11, businesses and organizations are routinely including a presence on social media sites as part of their marketing efforts. Businesses use these free social platforms to raise awareness of their brands, products, or services to those who elect to follow them. By following businesses, you get to see whatever content they upload, such as articles, press releases, images and announcements of products, or insider offers like deals and coupons. And, of course, companies are well aware that those who follow companies also have family, friends, and colleagues who "follow" them. Clearly, the return on investment is appealing—maintaining the feeds takes minimal effort and content often can be easily recycled from one social network to another, meaning there are fewer costly marketing efforts. Social media offers one way for businesses to tackle marketing cheaply, which makes it especially advantageous for small businesses with limited to non-existent marketing budgets.

As shown in Figure 12-1 the growth in number of users and unique visits by user to Pinterest is exploding—in the final six months of 2011, Pinterest grew its number of users from less than 2 million to almost 12 million! Given that the majority of Pinterest users are pinning things they like and following others who like similar things, Pinterest offers a unique and valuable audience for the small business to access.

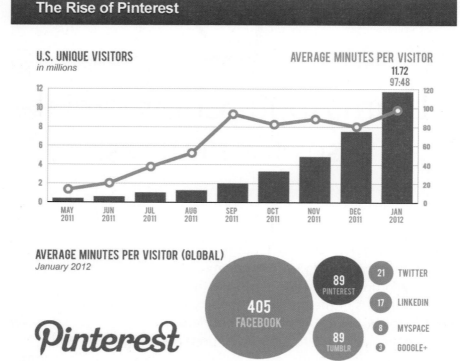

Figure 12-1 *Pinterest's growth in users during 2011. (Graphic used with permission from Statista Inc.)*

As you know by now, when people click pins they have the option to click through to the web site the content was sourced from. So, getting your business content on Pinterest can be excellent for driving traffic to your business web site or blog. In fact, it was reported by the online content-sharing website Shareaholic in February 2012 that Pinterest is ahead of Twitter, StumbleUpon, Bing, and Google+ in terms of traffic referral. Of course, it doesn't beat Google web search in the area of referrals, but from a marketing perspective, search engine optimization (SEO) is a much more involved process, and usually beyond the means of small businesses. That said, because users' pins can be created to link to your web site, this does add some SEO value to your company simply by getting your content on Pinterest.

The final selling point for using Pinterest for businesses is the way it can be integrated into your existing social networks, especially Facebook. It's possible for you to link your Pinterest account to your Facebook and Twitter accounts, widening your reach to those already within your existing social networks, and even further if they decide to comment or retweet your content (see "Control What You Post on Social Networks" in Chapter 3 for how to do this).

This chapter will focus on the key steps of how to get started using Pinterest for commercial purposes. We will look at creating boards that work for your business and how to connect Pinterest with your existing web site or blog. We will also look at making the content you have outside of Pinterest easily pinnable by adding features pointing to Pinterest. We will then look at ways to use your Pinterest boards to run an interesting and engaging marketing campaign. The final section will look at affiliate marketing—how Pinterest approaches this topic and ways you can use it to make money. These tips and explanations should leave you well placed to begin using Pinterest to your own financial advantage.

Create an Account and Boards for Your Business

The first step toward getting your business on Pinterest is creating an account for your business. You could use your personal account for this purpose, but it's worth noting that merging your personal and business presence might produce some unwanted noise for each audience.

When setting up an account for your business on Pinterest, remember to consider every step and text field through the eyes of your business, thinking how you would want potential customers to react when they read about you. This is a little tricky as Pinterest is set up for individuals rather than organizations, so while you can do many things in a straightforward way (like display your web site link, set up email preferences, and integrate company Twitter and Facebook feeds), some other things require a little more careful attention—most notably setting your display name and creating a description.

Carefully Consider Your
Display Name and Description

When setting your display name, it's a good idea to use your company name, splitting it over the first name and last name fields—most of the time Pinterest uses your full name in communication to or about you, but sometimes it uses only your first name. When writing your description, you will need to decide whether to write in the voice of your company or in your voice—this choice will depend on the nature of the business, so if you are trying to express the personal nature of your business, then you might like to choose first person, but other times third person may make more sense. Similarly, if you have a logo, this makes a good profile picture as this is more commonly identified with a business than a personal photo.

Explore What Other Brands Are Doing

Your first instinct might be to start pinning your product catalog, and this is something you may want to do at some point. But before you start, it's worth looking around to see what other businesses are doing—you will see that there is not one universal approach.

One immediate observation we made was that while many brands pin images of products they are selling, many also pin from other sources. This makes a lot of sense when you consider what the wider point of your Pinterest boards is—creating a company image and building a community of followers, not just creating an online catalog. Your boards can then become a place people come to for help and inspiration, as well as a source for driving users to your web site. It's worth remembering also that most of the time, customers wanting to browse a product catalog can already do that from a company web site. A great example of boards effectively pinning from various sources is Lowe's Home Improvement, which includes recipes, travel destinations, and kids' activities among their home improvement products.

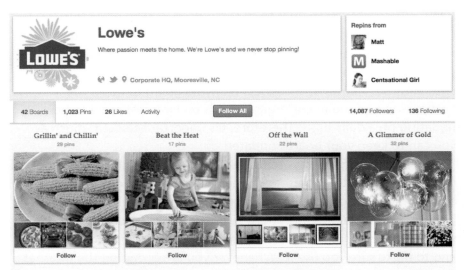

Pinning a variety of things from around the Internet can lead to stronger user-engagement as your brand becomes personalized and helps customers to identify with the business.

Let Customers and Followers Pin

Allowing people who follow you to pin to your boards is a great way to increase the reach of your boards, as the things they pin will be visible to those who follow their boards. It's a good idea to seek out power pinners with large followings as these people can really help in getting your content seen by the wider community. If you happen across any Pinterest members who are especially influential in your industry, these are great candidates to approach for this.

You do need to exercise some caution with this tactic because you don't want to open up your account to people who pin poor quality or irrelevant content. You also need to be careful in how you approach people; calling on people you don't know or with whom you have had only limited contact to pin to your boards may make some people uncomfortable and may appear as if you are spamming Pinterest.

Keep Your Boards Updated

Developing your community of followers is an ongoing process, but in addition to building you will need to think about retaining followers. One way to keep the door open for new followers and keep those you already have engaged is to ensure that you are constantly updating your boards with fresh content. Keeping pace with major corporations with large staff bases and budgets is always going to be an uphill battle—some of the major organizations on Pinterest seem to be updating on a daily basis. Therefore, it's important to do as much as you can to keep your boards updated.

There are plenty of ways to do this without having to spend time you don't have glued to a computer screen uploading images. A first step could be to work on integrating pinning into your daily Internet browsing. To make this as smooth as possible, it's important to make sure you have the Pin It bookmarklet installed on all of your computers, and to make sure you use it! Whenever you are browsing the Internet, try to pin often (but not obsessively)—it takes less than 30 seconds to pin something, and most likely there are things to pin on pages you were reading anyway. Another way to save time and keep things fresh is to use the Pinterest mobile app—you will be able to snap inspiring things, completed work, or new ideas and have them uploaded in a couple of minutes. You might also like to sign up with Pinerly (see Chapter 5), the online tool that can help you to automate some of your pinning.

Pin Engaging Images

This may seem like a really obvious thing to say, but we mention it only because so many people who use Pinterest for their business do not approach the site very differently from how they would a personal account. What draws people to Pinterest and what leads to high numbers of repins and glorious comment threads is interesting and engaging imagery. Unfortunately, many businesses simply pin their catalog photos with dull descriptions, which is a sure-fire way to bore an audience. Remember that new followers will not necessarily see you as a business when they first engage with your content; they will see you as another pinner, so try to make your pins the kinds of things people will want to share and comment on.

If your business makes products, you can use Pinterest pins to demonstrate how useful they are, rather than just show what they look like. A good way to accomplish this is by showing your products in use. It's also worth making sure your images are in high resolution to capture the fine details, and as colorful as possible—these qualities will make the images stand out. Figure 12-2 shows how one company successfully used bright, high-quality images of their products in use to engage and enthuse their audience.

Beach cover up

466 likes   22 comments
2127 repins

Figure 12-2 *A great example of how a colorful dynamic image from a small retailer went viral on Pinterest—2126 repins in 13 weeks!*

Make Sure Your Images Are Linked and Credited

When it comes to presenting images of your products, it's a good idea to make sure that they are linked back to your own web site. This will ensure that if users do click into your pins, they have somewhere to go at the end. It's possible for users to figure out where the image came from by clicking the pinner's profile and looking for a link there, but most users would probably not be inclined to put in the effort. If a user decides to click a pin, they will be expecting to be linked to the original piece of content, not left with nowhere to go.

If you are pinning images that aren't your products, it's always a good idea to make sure that the links point to the correct origin and that the owner is properly credited. While people using Pinterest for personal boards are unlikely to encounter any legal objections (remember sites have the option of blocking pins of their content), business owners should be a little more cautious. Big corporations can be very protective of their brand image, and employ large teams of lawyers specifically to search for and pursue any possible infringements. The cases that they bring can be very costly for those involved. That said, some businesses generate significant traffic through Pinterest for very little investment on their side and are unlikely to want to shut down that referral channel. Our general advice would be to trust your instincts here—if you have any reservations, then play it safe.

Try to Avoid Prices and Logos in Photos

Price tags can be great if you are using pins for your own reference, like we did with our boards on vacation choices and wish lists—they work because in those cases the cost was an important factor to consider. However, we would recommend avoid using price tags for your business boards because they make images less attractive and therefore intrinsically less pin-worthy for many users. Logos added onto your photos will have the same effect; they will distract users and take away from the aesthetic value of the image, making them less likely to be repinned.

This really comes down to what you are trying to achieve with your boards and what Pinterest is good at doing for you. The majority of

Pinterest users don't come to the site to shop, they come to be inspired and enjoy great visual content. So treating your Pinterest account like an extension of your commercial web site is unlikely to be successful. Pinterest can truly help you to raise awareness of your brand and develop a community of followers, which can do wonders for getting your business known. It's true that some clicks and repins could lead to sales or conversions for you, but you should see this as upside potential, not the main aim of your boards. As stated in the previous section, linking your images correctly will ensure that visiting your site (where pricing would be available) is always an option for those looking to buy.

Consider Using the Gift Tag

Having just said that you should avoid using price tags, there are places for them, and using them selectively might generate some sales opportunities. If your business sells products, you might like to consider taking advantage of the gift tag option within Pinterest. As we saw before, whenever you add a dollar or pound quantity to a pin description, the price tag is added to the image. However, this is not all that happens. Every pin with a price tag is automatically tagged as a gift within Pinterest. It is then indexed in the gifts category under the category of its board and price range.

Our advice here would be to create a board only for gifts so they are clearly organized. But more importantly, try not to make the sale of your products the be-all and end-all of your Pinterest account. Pinterest is much better at generating awareness and building a following than converting clicks into sales.

Make Pins and Boards Discoverable in Search

The Pinterest search functionality is not especially complex as far as search algorithms go. When you search for something it will crawl through all of the available text fields in people's pins to return matches for you, filtered by pins, boards, or people. Therefore, there is a great opportunity for you to optimize your pins, boards, and profile to show up better in search.

To do this, you will need to spend a little more time on your pins' description fields to ensure they contain the kinds of wording people will search on. A good target to aim for is a catchy description that contains relevant keywords such as a product color, its generic name, and its category.

Add Buttons to Your Site

Aside from what you do on Pinterest with boards and pins for your business, there are some things you can do on your own web site to allow visitors to engage with you on Pinterest. It's easy to add buttons to enable following and pinning directly from your site. The upside of adding these buttons is that it will widen your potential audience from those that discover your content on Pinterest to people visiting your site in the course of regular browsing.

Add the Follow Button to Your Site

Follow buttons for social media can usually be found on the home page of most businesses and organizations. These buttons allow visitors to follow your updates on popular platforms like Twitter and Facebook; you may already have these on your own home page. If you are planning to get your business on Pinterest, you should consider adding the Pinterest button.

"Follow Button" for Websites

Click the button of your choosing below to select the HTML code to embed. Then, copy and paste the code onto your site where you'd like it to appear.

Follow me on *Pinterest*

Pinterest

<a href="http://pinterest.com/custommadeltd/"><img src="https://s

The follow buttons act similarly to any linked image on your site. They can be used inline with your content, or as part of a sidebar.

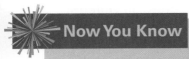

Now You Know **Adding the Follow Button to Your Site**

Pinterest lays out the instructions on how to add the follow button to your site on the help pages, under the Goodies menu. In order to add the button, you need to have access to your web site's HTML codebase. If you manage your own site, then this will be easy, but if you use a third party to manage your web site, you'll need to get them to do this.

1. Click About in the upper-right corner of the Pinterest page and select Help to go to the Pinterest help pages. Click Goodies on the left side of the page.

2. On the Goodies menu find the section entitled "Follow Button" for Web Sites.

3. Choose which of the four buttons you wish to use and click it. This will make the HTML appear, highlighted in blue in the box.

4. Copy the highlighted HTML code for that button and paste it into your site's HTML code in the position where you want it to appear.

Add the Pin It Button to Your Images

Whereas the follow button allows users to subscribe to content feeds, meaning they will see all of the new content you pin, the Pin It button allows users to pin your images directly without having to use the Pin It bookmarklet. It is important to remember that people who use the Internet have become accustomed to having everything made easy for them, so making it convenient to share your content is a logical approach to take, but the number of sharing icons available these days can be overwhelming, so it's important for you to decide which ones are most important to include on your site. If you are making an effort to increase brand awareness and promote your business on Pinterest, then it makes sense to include the Pin It button.

Add a Pin It button to invite your readers to pin your work onto Pinterest.

The Pin It button is made to look and feel like the Facebook and Twitter buttons your readers already use. For best results, place the Pin It button near your other social sharing tools.

URL of the page to pin (required, start with http):

http://www.custommade-uk.co.uk/balustrades-7.html

URL of the image to pin (required, start with http):

made-uk.co.uk/core/gallery/large/c7-1329057221.jpg

Description of the page to be pinned:

Beautiful glass balustrade

Descriptions are optional but recommended; they will make pinning much easier for your users.

Pin Count [Horizontal ◆]

Pin it 5

Add this link to your page, right where you want the button to appear:

```
<a href="http://pinterest.com/pin/create/button/?url=http%3A%2F
%2Fwww.custommade-uk.co.uk%2Fbalustrades-7.html&media=http%3A%2F
%2Fwww.custommade-uk.co.uk%2Fcore%2Fgallery%2Flarge%2Fc7-1329057221.jpg&
description=Bueautiful%20glass%20ballustarde" class="pin-it-button" count-
layout="horizontal"><img border="0" src="//assets.pinterest.com/images/PinExt.png"
title="Pin It" /></a>
```

Add this code to your page only once, directly above the closing </BODY> tag:

```
<script type="text/javascript" src="//assets.pinterest.com/js/pinit.js"></script>
```

Important: you can have as many Pin It buttons on a page as you like, but you only need to include the JavaScript once!

 **Now You Know** **Adding the Pin It Button to Your Site**

Pinterest lays out the instructions for adding the Pin It button in the Goodies menu. Again, you will need to have access to your web site's HTML codebase.

1. Click About in the upper-right corner of the Pinterest page and select Help to go to the Pinterest help pages. Click Goodies on the left side of the page.

2. On the Goodies menu find the section entitled Pin It Button for Web Sites.

3. Add the URL of the page to pin (the page on which you want the button to appear) and the URL of the image to pin. Type the text you want to appear in the description field when the user pins.

4. You will see two sets of HTML code generated in the boxes below the URL and description fields. The first piece should be pasted wherever you wish the button to appear—this can be multiple times on the same page. The second piece is JavaScript code that only needs to pasted once into each page where the button appears, just after the closing body tag (</body>).

Run a Pinterest Campaign

Any visit to Facebook will show you that marketing campaigns in social media are extremely popular. Their successes can be hard to document because the success metrics can be very different. In terms of running a Pinterest campaign for a small business, you probably aren't going to be able to measure it in terms of revenue increase. Your best way to judge a Pinterest marketing campaign is by the number of interactions you see around your boards, as these represent some form of customer engagement. Once you get your account set up on Pinterest and have a good number of followers, you might want to think about running some sort of campaign to see if you can increase awareness of your brand.

This section will look at the most popular type of marketing campaign that is often run on Pinterest—the board-creation competition. The real life examples we will look at are all run by large corporate organizations with help from advertising agencies, but we talk about how the basic idea can be used by a business of any size to help raise awareness of a product or brand with a realistic investment in terms of time and money.

Run a Board-Creation Competition

The basic premise of this idea is to have your followers create boards related to your brand or product in some way. A winner can be determined and a prize can be given. Most notably this type of campaign has been run by clothing brands Guess and Lands' End, who offered very appealing prizes to their winners. But the real beauty of this type of campaign is that it requires minimal effort on the business-owner's part to start and run.

Planning the Campaign

First up, you might solicit advice from any legal advisers you have, in order to make sure the campaign is safe to run. You would also want to post some kind of disclaimer to cover yourself against claims of liability. Beyond that, the basics you will need to have in place before you can start your campaign are the type of boards you want people to create, the rules of the competition, and the prize you are going to offer. In the campaign run by Guess, they asked entrants to make a board themed on one of their new season colors. Each entrant's board had to start with a repin from the Guess competition board, and there had to be at least five pins (with a given hashtag included in each pin) on your final entry board. The winners each received a pair of Guess jeans.

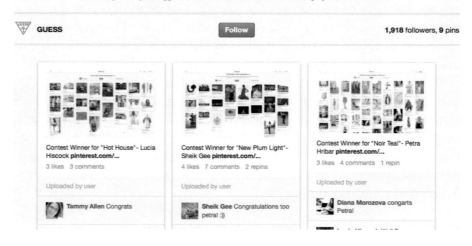

It sounds very complicated, but really it isn't. What you are setting your entrants up with is instructions for what to do, giving them a pin to get started with, and telling them what they can win.

Launching the Campaign

In order to keep the campaign from overflowing all of your boards, you should set up a campaign board. You can use the board description to outline the details of the campaign, as well as set start and end dates and judging criteria to determine the winner—it could be a random draw, chosen by a nominated individual, or based on the number of repins their own board generates.

Your first pin should really be a completion rules pin, where you outline the procedure and rules more clearly. If you don't have design skills to make this type of pin yourself, you could use Pinstamatic or another third-party service that allows text to be turned into an image. Your pin should do the following:

- Instruct people who wish to enter to follow you on Pinterest.

- Tell people how to get started—a good way is by repinning something from your competition board to the board they are creating (you can ask them to repin the completion rules pin for this purpose). You could also specify what the board should be named, which is a way to get your brand to show more results in search.

- Tell people what to pin on their boards—this will depend on the type of competition you are running, but you should also create a hashtag for the promotion.

- Tell people how to submit their boards—most campaigns like this ask users to post a link to their board in the comments field of the rules pin.

Something ModCloth. Something You

You're Invited!

Enter to win a $100 GC, and inspire ModCloth's 2012 spring wedding campaign.

1. Something vintage
2. Something new
3. Something handmade
4. Something blue
5. Color theme
6. Invite inspiration
7. A lovely location
8. Vintage style icon
9. Floral arrangement(s)
10. The perfect 'do
11. Makeup or nails
12. The perfect ModCloth shoe for you
13. Matching ModCloth accessories
14. ModCloth bridesmaid dresses
15. ModCloth party favors
16. Table setting theme
17. Sweet eats or savory treats
18. A traditional or non-traditional cake
19. A creative cocktail
20. Something you

Take part in our first themed contest on @Pinterest! To enter, create a board, title it "Spring ModCloth Wedding," then add a description of your aesthetic to your board. Make sure your board contains each of the 20 pins listed above, in no particular order. In each pin's caption, include the number, and name that the pin corresponds to for the contest, along with the hashtags #modcloth and #wedding . When your board is perfect, share it with us by posting a comment on the original contest announcement pin, with a link to your board, located in our

Finishing the Campaign

Once the end date has arrived, you should adjust your board and rules descriptions to state that the promotion is over and thank everyone for their entries. After you have reviewed all of your entries, you will need to announce the winner. A good way to do this is to take a screenshot of the winning board and upload that image to your competition board with a caption congratulating the winner and detailing when the prize will be sent.

Make Money from Pinterest

As stated earlier in the chapter, getting your business onto Pinterest can be great for increasing awareness, but it isn't necessarily great at generating income for you. In this section we focus on how it's actually possible to make money from Pinterest—primarily through *affiliate marketing*.

It should be said from the outset, that affiliate marketing is a hugely competitive business, and the rewards can be small. However, as we will show you, it can be fun to have pins with the potential to earn cash, and it's reasonably easy to do. Although the income increments might be small, those small amounts of cash can accumulate over time, making your efforts worthwhile.

In this section, we will explain the basics of affiliate marketing, how Pinterest currently uses it, and how you can use it in your daily pinning to add a little income potential to your work.

Understand Affiliate Marketing

Affiliate marketing is a way in which retail businesses let other people or organizations market their goods for them. The retail business then pays the person or organization a commission based on any sales that they generate. It's a fairly complex business in terms of how the technicalities of it work, but basically there are four key players in the affiliate marketing workflow:

- **The Retailer** This is the organization that is actually selling the item.

- **The Network** An intermediary that operates between retailers and affiliates by hosting different offers for the affiliate to choose from. They also manage payments to the affiliate.
- **The Affiliate** The person or organization that is promoting the retailer's goods.
- **The Customer** Any person making a purchase of the goods sold by the retailer.

It's worth noting that sometimes there are only three players in the scenario. If a site runs its own affiliate program, you can dispense with the network and deal directly with the site itself. Examples of retailers that run their own affiliate marketing programs are Amazon, Best Buy, and Barnes & Noble. Figure 12-3 shows the cycle of affiliate marketing.

As an example, let's say you write a blog on the subject of soccer and frequently recommend equipment and post images and links to places

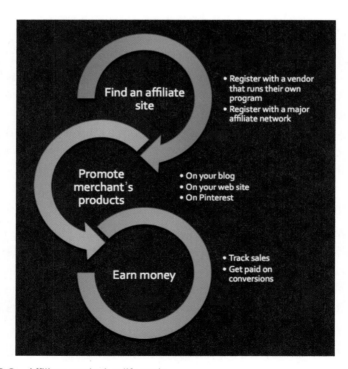

Figure 12-3 *Affiliate marketing life cycle*

where readers can buy them. Rather than just using the URL and image you can get through browsing the retailer's site, you can sign up for their affiliate program. Within this program you will be given a different (longer) URL to post in your site. The difference between the URLs looks like this (using Amazon as an example):

Regular Internet URL: http://www.amazon.com/dp/0743273567
Affiliate URL: http://www.amazon.com/dp/0743273567/?tag=assoc-id-20

This second URL contains code that is associated with your affiliate account. When a user clicks that link, they are taken to that item's page on Amazon where they could purchase it—this is seamless for the user and they will not be aware of any difference in the page they land on. However, Amazon will know instantly that this referral came from you because it came via the longer affiliate URL containing the affiliate ID. If the user purchases the item, you get a small cut of the transaction.

The retailer makes their content available to a network (unless they have their own self-administered affiliate program). The affiliates grab links from the network. Customers click the links on the affiliates' sites and buy things. The customer pays the retailer, who pays a cut to the network, who pays a cut to the affiliate.

How Pinterest Uses Affiliate Marketing

Currently, Pinterest does not have any large revenue streams—they do not accept paid ads from sponsors, nor do they directly promote commercial content. This will undoubtedly change if and when the company decides to go public.

Right now, Pinterest's largest revenue generator is affiliate linking, and this is a topic of some controversy that has been widely reported in the press. The vast majority of people who pin on Pinterest from the Internet do so using the Pin It bookmarklet, and do not use affiliate linking in their pins. For these pins, Pinterest uses a third-party service to add its own affiliate links to those pins (overwriting the shorter URL captured when the pinner created the pin). The service, provided by a company called Skimlinks, crawls the Pinterest site looking for URLs that are eligible for an affiliate link but currently do not have one. When they find an eligible URL, they replace it with the longer affiliate URL (like we saw earlier in this chapter) so Pinterest will earn any commission coming from a purchase on that referral.

So why is this controversial? Some people have argued that Pinterest should not be altering people's pins in such a covert way. However, others (including Pinterest) counter this by saying there is no disruption at all to the user experience and most people will not notice. It's also worth stating that Pinterest's policy is only to overwrite URLs that are eligible for an affiliate link and do not have one—they do not overwrite affiliate links added by users with their own affiliate link. For our ten cents, we would argue that users not adding affiliate links probably have no interest in affiliate marketing. If Pinterest is able to generate some income without affecting user experience, then it seems fair game.

Use Affiliate Marketing Yourself on Pinterest

Using affiliate marketing on Pinterest yourself can be reasonably straightforward, depending on how involved you want to get. The procedure is pretty much the same as normal pinning, but there are two additional steps—acquiring the affiliate link, and adding that link to your pin.

The easiest way to begin is to sign up for an affiliate program at a vendor you like to pin things from (assuming they have one). If they do not have a program listed on their site, they may operate exclusively through a network like Commission Junction or Google Affiliate Network. These programs are free to sign up for and have very intuitive interfaces to negotiate. Once you are registered you can begin using the service—although the numerous program sites differ somewhat, they all offer some facility for you to search for the product you wish to promote. Once you find it, you will be given the longer URL. This URL then needs to be added to your pin.

Now You Know **Adding an Affiliate Link to Your Pin**

Your two steps are implied in the title here—you need to pin the product you are looking to promote and you need to find if there is an affiliate link available either from a retailer directly or an affiliate network. If there is, you are in business! You can then copy that link. Once you have done this, use the option to view the pin you wish to promote, and then the option to edit it. You will see a box labeled URL to the left of the image, along with the other details of the pin. The URL box will contain the link from which you pinned the image. Simply delete this URL and paste in the affiliate link you copied earlier. Save the changes and you are done!

Index